The
SOUP SISTERS
and
BROTH BROTHERS
Cookbook

Barley, Red Bean and Spinach Soup (see page 19)

The
SOUP SISTERS
and
BROTH BROTHERS
Cookbook

More Than 100 Heart-Warming Seasonal Recipes
for You to Cook at Home

Edited by
SHARON HAPTON

appetite
by RANDOM HOUSE

Appetite by Random House colophon is a registered trademark

Library and Archives of Canada Cataloguing in Publication is available upon request
ISBN: 978-0-449-01642-8
eBook ISBN: 978-0-449-01643-5

Cover and text design: Leah Springate
Cover image: Shallon Cunningham, Salt Photography
Food photography and styling: Julie Van Rosendaal
Snowflakes on page 61: © Vanias | Dreamstime.com

Printed and bound in China

Published in Canada by Appetite by Random House,
a division of Random House of Canada Limited,
a Penguin Random House company

www.randomhouse.ca

10 9 8 7 6 5 4 3 2 1

Pear, Parsnip and Celeriac Soup with Pumpkin Seed Salsa Verde (see page 38)

CONTENTS

Yemenite Chicken Soup (see page 188)

A Hug in a Bowl

It's been two years since the publication of our first cookbook. I am profoundly grateful to you—our thousands of Canadian supporters and volunteers—and to Random House for helping make it a best-seller! The proceeds from sales have helped us to keep the soup flowing. *The Soup Sisters Cookbook* was such a success, I'm thrilled we're launching *The Soup Sisters and Broth Brothers Cookbook*, packed with 114 of our favorite new soup recipes donated by volunteers, chefs and food celebrities from across Canada.

As in our first book, here you'll find soups for fall, winter, spring and summer so that, whatever the season, there's a soup to suit. If you're a newbie soup maker, you'll want to check out the tips and techniques up front. Most of the recipes serve between four and eight people, depending, of course, on the size of your appetite. Soup leftovers are perfect for freezing and we've included instructions for how to do that, too.

The Soup Sisters organization has been on an incredible journey of growth and evolution since our first book was published. In more than 20 cities across Canada, women (Soup Sisters) and men (Broth Brothers) are now cooking up about 10,000 servings of soup each month for women, children and youth in crisis.

Soup Sisters has a twofold mandate: to nurture and nourish women and children whose lives have been affected by domestic abuse and family violence, and to provide soup for youth aged 16 to 24 who are transitioning from street culture into mainstream society.

Anonymity is critically important in the shelters that help women and children who are escaping domestic violence, so we have little direct contact with those recipients. But we know from shelter managers and support staff that the soup is warming not only the stomachs but also the hearts of those often facing the worst crisis in their lives.

The youth we support write us beautiful and heartwarming letters. They even request their favorite soups. It's so satisfying to know that our gesture of support and message of care have earned their trust. The soup we make is not a form of "charity." It's offered as a sign of respect that recognizes the determination, strength and integrity of young people who are moving from survival on the streets to independence in mainstream society.

Soup Sisters and Broth Brothers believe in the potential of all young people. We send them this message with every bowl of soup we deliver. We hope this form of nurturing helps them on their journey to build a better life for themselves. We strive to debunk the myths surrounding young people on the streets and are honored to have the opportunity to let them know they matter.

One of the agencies we support is The Doorway in Calgary, an organization dedicated to helping young people leave street life. According to the agency's executive director, Marilyn Dyck, the soups we deliver each month have provided warmth and nourishment, welcomed youth in stormy and calm weather, generated conversations between participants and volunteers, and been taken home by young people to comfort them when a paycheck is just barely enough to pay the rent.

As Marilyn told me: "Soup from Soup Sisters and Broth Brothers provides healthy, warm meals and is a token of your commitment to young people. It also gives The Doorway a valued opportunity to meet with Calgarians who share a passion for young people." That our intention is received and understood as we intend is the greatest gift Soup Sisters and Broth Brothers could ever get.

When I launched Soup Sisters in 2009, I had no idea that such a simple idea would put me at the helm of a thriving national organization. I no longer have time to make soup at home! I never imagined that providing a "hug in a bowl" would extend so far beyond the care and comfort contained in each delicious serving.

Soup Sisters and Broth Brothers have provided a familiar and friendly environment— the kitchen—for conversation and awareness on domestic violence, bringing this issue to the attention of thousands of people in the communities in which we operate. In the process, I've learned a lot, too. I've learned that busy people are still hungry for a hands-on way to contribute if they're offered a manageable time frame. When they see the results of just one evening's teamwork—all those pots of hearty soup—they know they've made a tangible difference in people's lives and had fun doing it. The experience leaves a lasting impression that often entices their friends and family to join us for an evening or two.

I've learned that men and women are equally innately nurturing. Our Broth Brothers have become an integral and valuable part of our soup-making events across the country. Men tend to the soup with great commitment and concern, and I'm gratified that they find our events inclusive and welcoming. In this way, we've become a safe place for men to take a public stand on ending violence against women and families.

Finally, I've learned that our volunteers have a deeper commitment than even I realized. They never leave our ranks without finding someone to step into their shoes. Imagine a world where people cherished their importance as a part of something bigger, so that leaving was only an option when they knew someone would take care of things as well as they did.

Every month our volunteers guarantee that fresh soup will be delivered to provide nourishing comfort to someone in crisis. These dedicated men and women have become more than volunteers to me. I consider them true friends of the highest order, and I thank them for their dedication and friendship.

In this book our volunteers have shared their rich perspectives on the making, sharing and giving of soup (It's More Than Just Soup, page 193). I think that, at some point, the soup maker and the soup recipient become one. We all need nurturing and we all need to nurture others.

At Soup Sisters we believe that wherever there is a shelter for women, children or youth in crisis, there should be a Soup Sisters chapter. Sadly, shelters exist everywhere, in cities large and small. But fortunately, caring men and women are there, too, looking to make a tangible difference to individual lives and to the larger issues of tackling violence against women and children, and giving youth at risk a chance. If you would like to start a local chapter, please contact us at info@soupsisters.org.

Yours in soup,

Sharon Hapton
Founder, Soup Sisters and Broth Brothers

Getting Started

If your pantry, vegetable basket and fridge are fully stocked, it's easy to make soup at a moment's notice. Here are our tips for what you'll need.

The Pantry

A well-stocked pantry is like having a proper first aid kit. With these essentials, everything you need is waiting for you right there in your kitchen, any time you want to stir up some soup.

Beans, lentils and split peas

Having canned beans on hand makes it much simpler to whip up a batch of soup fast. We do, however, like to keep a variety of dried beans in the pantry, too. Dried beans need to be soaked before cooking. Here's how to do it:

1. Pick over the beans to check for any grit, then rinse and drain them.

2. Put the beans in a large pot and add enough water to cover them by 1 inch (2.5 cm).

3. Cover with a lid and let the beans soak overnight. Alternatively, bring the beans to a boil and boil over high heat for 2 minutes. Remove the pot from the heat, cover and let stand for 1 hour.

4. Drain the beans well before using in a recipe.

Dried lentils and split peas don't need to be soaked before using, and they cook more quickly than beans. Because of the heartiness they add to any soup, they're also great to have on hand.

Oils

Canola, sunflower, grapeseed or regular olive oils are all great for frying. Keep your good fruity extra virgin olive oil for drizzling on top of a soup or dipping your bread in.

Rice and pasta

Assorted types of rice add variety to your soup making: arborio can thicken a bisque; brown rice can beef up a chili. And pasta in a variety of shapes and sizes is sure to add diversity, too: toss a few handfuls of macaroni into a pot of minestrone, or add alphabet-shaped pasta to a soup to serve to your kids.

Salt and pepper

Unless the recipe says otherwise, we use kosher salt and freshly ground black pepper in the soups in this book. When salting a soup, remember that you can add salt but you can't take it out. Add salt to taste just before serving because, if you salt the soup perfectly halfway through cooking and the stock reduces, you'll end up with a salty soup. Add salt a little at a time, stir the soup and then taste it, repeating these steps until the soup tastes just right.

Adding pepper to taste is similar to adding salt, but the effect of pepper takes a little longer to permeate, so wait a couple of minutes before you taste the soup. Better still, just put the pepper grinder on the table and let folks help themselves.

Spices and Herbs

With the following herbs and spices in your pantry, you can make any of the soups in this book:

- Aleppo pepper flakes* (see page 112)
- allspice, ground
- basil leaves, dried
- bay leaves
- Cajun blackening spice (see page 178)
- cardamom pods (whole)
- cardamom, ground
- cayenne
- chili powder
- cinnamon sticks
- cinnamon, ground
- cloves (whole)
- coriander seeds (whole)
- coriander, ground
- cumin seeds (whole)
- cumin, ground
- curry leaves, dried
- curry powder, mild, medium or hot
- fenugreek seeds
- ginger, ground
- Italian herb seasoning, dried
- Marash chili*, crushed (see page 21)
- Mexican oregano leaves*, dried
- mint leaves, dried
- mustard seeds, black
- nutmeg (ground nutmeg or whole nutmeg to freshly grate)
- oregano leaves, dried
- paprika, Hungarian sweet
- paprika, Spanish hot smoked*
- paprika, Spanish sweet smoked
- parsley leaves, dried
- pepper, Espelette* (see page 153)

- peppercorns, black (whole)
- peppercorns, white (whole)
- red chili flakes
- red chilies, dried (whole)
- rosemary, dried
- saffron threads
- star anise (whole)
- tarragon leaves, dried
- thyme leaves, dried
- turmeric
- za'atar (see page 112)
- * denotes an ingredient for which an alternative is given in the recipe

Stock

On pages 10–12 you'll find easy recipes for making stocks from scratch. However, if you're short of time, keep some store-bought stock in your cupboard, too—we prefer the organic varieties. If you're really stuck, use stock cubes. Just remember that ready-made stock and stock cubes usually contain a lot of sodium, so you'll need to add less salt.

The Vegetable Basket

Be sure to always have carrots, celery and onions on hand. They all keep for a long time and if they start to look a little bit limp, that's when they're perfect for tossing into a batch of stock (see pages 10–12).

Squash (especially butternut) and root vegetables, like potatoes and rutabaga, will keep most of the winter in a cool, dry cupboard, so they're especially handy to have if you get snowed in.

Garlic is a must-have, too. If you end up with little green sprouts poking out of the top of the bulb, don't worry, you can pop those in the stockpot, too.

The Fridge/Freezer

Not every soup ingredient will be waiting for you in the pantry. Fresh, vibrant flavor often comes from ingredients such as the following that need to be stored in the fridge or freezer.

Bacon

Few ingredients can elevate soup to the next level as quickly as bacon. You can add it to the pot when you're making homemade stock (see pages 10–12), cook with bacon's rendered fat (instead of using oil or butter) or top your soup with crunchy bacon bits.

Butter

For best flavor, use unsalted butter in cooking— you can always add more salt to taste.

Frozen stock

When you've made a big batch of homemade stock (see pages 10–12), it's a great idea to freeze some so you can make beautiful, from-scratch soup anytime you like. For tips on how to freeze soup and stock, turn to page 8.

Herbs

The beautiful bright flavor of fresh herbs is hard to beat, although dried herbs can be used in a pinch.

Fresh parsley, cilantro and basil are lovely when finely chopped and stirred into your soups at the last minute. Keep fresh herbs in your vegetable crisper or, if you have a green thumb, grow them on your windowsill.

Lemons

Lemons come with two awesome ingredients in one nifty yellow package. You can use a zester or Microplane grater to remove the powerfully aromatic zest from the outside of a lemon, and then squeeze the fruit to harvest the tart lemon juice inside.

Essential Equipment

Blender

A blender is essential for puréeing soup and produces a much smoother result than a food processor. Your best choice is either a countertop blender or an immersion blender.

A countertop blender is the kind with a goblet that sits on a motorized base. Choose a blender that has progressive speeds so you can slowly turn up the dial to get the smoothest of purées.

A cheaper option is an immersion blender (sometimes called a hand blender or wand blender). This is the kind you submerge in a pot of soup, switch on and move around in the pot to purée the soup. An immersion blender takes longer to purée a soup, and the soup may not be perfectly smooth as with a countertop blender. On the plus side, immersion blenders are easy to clean and fun to swirl around.

Read up on soup puréeing tips on page 8.

Cheesecloth

Cheesecloth is handy for tying up little bouquet garni bundles (see page 39). It's also useful for lining a sieve when you want to strain the teensiest impurities out of your stock.

Cutting boards

Softwood or plastic cutting boards are best because glass, marble or hard composite boards will dull your knives.

Knives

Dull knives are dangerous because they slip around and you don't know where they're going to go. A sharp knife goes where you tell it to and ensures you get nice, even cuts, so you'll get nice, even cooking. Invest in good knives and learn how to sharpen them.

Pots

Heavy-bottomed stainless steel pots and saucepans make the soup world go round. The thicker the bottom of the pot, the better it will conduct heat and the more control you'll have over browning vegetables and boiling soup. It's helpful to have a variety of sizes of pots and saucepans so you can make big batches of stock or soup, or reheat small portions of soup for dinner.

Sieve

A large fine-mesh sieve is useful for straining impurities out of stock and for ensuring puréed soups are as smooth as can be.

Vegetable peelers

Peelers come in many shapes and sizes. The fastest and most efficient is the Y-shaped or speed peeler. Get one with a good grip and it will peel anything very effectively.

Soup-Making Techniques

How to purée soup

Some soups are meant to be chunky, some should be smooth as silk. Here's how to achieve a velvety potful.

...with a countertop blender

1. Remove the center cap from the blender lid. This is to let the steam from the hot soup escape. An airtight lid combined with steam pressure and a whirling propeller is primed to make a dangerously hot mess.
2. Fill your blender only halfway with equal parts soup chunks and liquid.
3. Put the lid on the blender and place a folded dry dishcloth over the hole where the center cap was so that nothing will splatter out. You can quite safely place your hand on the cloth to hold the lid while you're puréeing the soup.
4. Start the blender on low speed and slowly bring it up to full tilt.
5. Blend until the soup is smooth, then pour it into a large pitcher or bowl.
6. Continue blending the soup in small batches until it is all silky smooth.
7. When all the soup is blended, rinse out the soup pot and return the blended soup to the pot. For super-smooth soup, pour it back into the clean pot through a fine-mesh sieve.

...with an immersion blender

1. Place the end of the immersion blender into the soup, right to the bottom of the pot, then turn it on.
2. Move the immersion blender around the bottom of the pot to ensure there are no splatters.
3. You can even tilt the pot and work the blender around in the deep end.
4. When you think it's smooth enough, keep going for 5 more minutes so it gets even smoother.

How to chill and freeze soup and stock

It's very important to know how to store hot soup and stock properly. If you simply put a big pot of hot soup in your fridge or freezer, the soup will warm everything up and cause other foods to spoil.

To chill a big pot of soup or stock, you'll need lots of ice.

1. Put the plug in a clean kitchen sink. Place your pot of hot soup in the sink. Add ice to the sink to come one-quarter of the way up the side of the pot. If it's winter, and it might be if you're making soup, you can use freshly fallen snow instead of ice.
2. Fill the sink with cold water from the tap until it reaches the same level as the soup in the pot. Keep stirring the soup until it cools down to about lukewarm or body temperature.
3. Transfer the soup to smaller containers and store them in the fridge or freezer.

If you want to freeze a soup that calls for cream and/or pasta, prepare the soup without these ingredients, then freeze the soup. After thawing the soup, add the cream and/or pasta and continue with the recipe.

A Key to the Icons

Throughout this book you'll discover the following icons, designed to help you get to the heart of the recipe with just a quick glance:

 Vegetarian soups might include eggs and/or dairy products, so check the recipe carefully if these are foods you'd rather live without.

 Vegan soups are derived from vegetables or grains; they are free of all dairy products and eggs (although some soups might call for optional non-vegan garnishes). Vegan soups are also suitable for vegetarians.

 Gluten-free soups contain no flour products, whole grains or bread. Some may contain items, such as soy sauce or stock, that are available in gluten-free formats, so be sure to read the ingredients on the jar, bottle or package before you buy.

 A wooden spoon indicates a helpful hint or tip that gives you a little more detail about the recipe; for example, a serving suggestion or information on alternative ingredients.

A soup bowl highlights a story, tip or tale that comes directly from the chef, food professional, Soup Sister or Broth Brother who contributed the recipe.

Classic Comforting Stocks

Homemade stock is the secret to making the best homemade soups. With a little bit of effort, you can include completely from-scratch soups in your repertoire. Creating a stock portfolio is a great way to diversify your soup offerings. Fix a variety of stocks when you have time and then keep them in your freezer—you'll be ready to simmer up delicious, from-scratch soup whenever you feel like it!

Vegetable Stock

Makes about 24 cups (6 L)

Vegetable stocks are handy to have tucked away in the freezer because making vegetarian soups then becomes a cinch. In addition, the stock's light flavor won't overwhelm whatever ingredients you add to the soup.

24 cups (6 L) cold water (approx.)
2 carrots, peeled and diced
2 onions, finely chopped
2 stalks celery, diced
2 cloves garlic

3 sprigs parsley
1 sprig fresh thyme
2 bay leaves
10 whole black peppercorns

1. Combine all the ingredients in a large pot. The water should cover everything in the pot. If it doesn't, add more water until everything is submerged.

2. Bring to a boil, uncovered, over high heat. When the water boils, reduce the heat to medium.

3. Boil gently for 1 hour, never letting the stock boil vigorously. But, unlike with meat and fish stocks, you can still boil vegetable stock quite rapidly because there are no proteins to make the stock cloudy. So you'll be done much more quickly.

4. Line a fine-mesh sieve with a double layer of cheesecloth. Ladle the stock and solids through the sieve into a large bowl or a clean pot. Discard the solids and use the stock immediately, or freeze it in small containers for future use (see page 8).

Chicken, Turkey or Beef Stock

Makes about 24 cups (6 L)

24 cups (6 L) cold water (approx.)
5 lb (2.2 kg) chicken or turkey bones
  or 8 lb (3.5 kg) beef bones
1 carrot, peeled and diced
1 onion, finely chopped
1 stalk celery, diced

2 cloves garlic
3 sprigs parsley
2 bay leaves
1 sprig thyme
10 whole black peppercorns
2 whole cloves

1. Combine all the ingredients in a large pot. The water should cover everything in the pot. If it doesn't, add more water until everything is submerged.

2. Bring to a boil, uncovered, over high heat. As soon as you see any bubbles break the surface, reduce the heat to a bare simmer.

3. Simmer, uncovered, for 2 hours, never letting the stock boil. Boiling will cause the proteins to coagulate and come out of the bones and will result in a cloudy stock. If the boiling gets away from you, though, and you do end up with a cloudy stock, feel free to still use it. Cloudy stocks are not the end of the world—they're just not as pretty as clear stocks.

4. While the stock simmers ever so gently, use a large metal spoon to occasionally skim off any impurities that float to the surface.

5. Line a fine-mesh sieve with a double layer of cheesecloth. Ladle the stock and solids through the sieve into a large bowl or a clean pot. Discard the solids and use the stock immediately, or freeze it in small containers for future use (see page 8).

Brown Stock

To add depth of flavor and color to your stock, take the bones, carrots and onions from the Chicken, Turkey or Beef Stock recipe, spread them out in a large roasting pan and roast them in a 450°F (230°C) oven for about 45 minutes or until they are very dark brown.

Good proper stock is something you should make from scratch at least once, so you can discover just how easy it is and how much better it tastes than store-bought stock or stock cubes. Once you've tried it, you won't want to go back!

You can use raw chicken bones (from chicken portions you've boned out) or cooked chicken bones (from the Sunday roast). Or, buy meaty beef bones (preferably those that contain marrow) from your butcher.

Fish Stock

Makes about 24 cups (6 L)

24 cups (6 L) cold water (approx.)
5 lb (2.2 kg) fish bones or fresh fish heads (gills removed)
1 carrot, peeled and diced
1 onion, finely chopped
1 stalk celery, diced
2 cloves garlic
3 sprigs parsley
2 bay leaves
1 sprig fresh thyme
10 whole black peppercorns

This is one stock you want to make fresh and use right away. Frozen fish stock from the store or even frozen homemade isn't all that great, so make it fresh and use it immediately. The good news: it takes way less time than meat stock.

If you don't have fish bones and heads on hand (and who does?), buy them from your fish store. Avoid using bones and heads from oily fish (like salmon and mackerel) as these will make your stock cloudy.

1. Combine all the ingredients in a large pot. The water should cover everything in the pot. If it doesn't, add more water until everything is submerged.

2. Bring to a boil, uncovered, over high heat. As soon as you see any bubbles break the surface, reduce the heat to a bare simmer.

3. Simmer, uncovered, for 20 to 30 minutes, never letting the stock boil. Boiling will cause the proteins to coagulate and come out of the bones and will result in a cloudy stock. If the boiling gets away from you, though, and you do end up with a cloudy stock, feel free to still use it. Cloudy stocks are not the end of the world—they're just not as pretty as clear stocks.

4. While the stock simmers ever so gently, use a large metal spoon to occasionally skim off any impurities that float to the surface.

5. Line a fine-mesh sieve with a double layer of cheesecloth. Ladle the stock and solids through the sieve into a large bowl or a clean pot. Discard the solids and use the stock immediately.

ellini Soup
card, onion, garlic,
vegetable stock, oil,

FALL

When autumn chases away the last warm days of summer, Soup Sisters and Broth Brothers kick into high gear. To celebrate, we dust off our heartier soup recipes and start to add a bit of warming spice to the stockpot. Many fall vegetables make wonderful soups, producing bowlfuls as colorful as the changing leaves—in gorgeous shades of deep orange, red or gold.

In this chapter, you'll find recipes starring the very best of the season's harvest, with apples, squash and even peanuts in the leading roles. There are special-occasion soups, such as Lobster Cappuccino, for memorable events, and everyday soups, too, such as Potato-Cheddar, for those times when a quick meal is needed.

You'll be sure to reach for these recipes when the temperatures start to dip.

Apple-Parsnip Cream with Chorizo Sausage

Liana Robberecht, Executive Chef, Calgary Petroleum Club

Makes about 4 servings

¼ cup (60 mL) butter
2 Gala apples, peeled, cored and diced
2 cups (500 mL) peeled and diced
  parsnips
½ large onion, finely chopped
2 Tbsp (30 mL) finely chopped shallots
2 Tbsp (30 mL) minced roasted red
  pepper
1 Tbsp (15 mL) minced roasted garlic
1½ tsp (7 mL) peeled and grated fresh
  ginger
½ tsp (2 mL) ground allspice

¼ tsp (1 mL) dried thyme leaves
2½ cups (625 mL) chicken stock
1 cup (250 mL) whipping cream
  (35% MF)
½ cup (125 mL) vermouth
½ cup (125 mL) olive oil
Juice of 1 lemon
1 fresh (uncooked) chorizo sausage,
  casing removed
1 tsp (5 mL) sea salt
1 tsp (5 mL) pepper

1. In a large pot, melt the butter over medium heat. Add the apples, parsnips, onion, shallots, red pepper, garlic, ginger, allspice and thyme. Cook, stirring often, until the onion has softened.

2. Add the stock and cream and bring to a boil.

3. Reduce the heat and simmer, covered, until the apples and parsnips are tender, about 20 minutes.

4. Purée the soup until smooth. Add the vermouth, olive oil and lemon juice. Reheat gently.

5. Meanwhile, crumble the chorizo sausage into a small skillet. Cook, stirring often, over medium heat until the sausage is cooked through. Drain on paper towels.

6. Season with salt and pepper to taste. Ladle into bowls and scatter the chorizo over the top.

Most of us associate soup with a treasured childhood memory of being cared for by a person who loves us very, very much. In my memory, that person is my mother. A bowl of her soup gave me the satisfied comfort I couldn't find anywhere else. Making soup is the perfect way to remember how it feels to have someone take care of you.

For vegetarians at your table, use vegetable stock instead of chicken and omit the chorizo. And for the lactose-intolerant, simply replace the cream with stock.

—Liana Robberecht

Apple, Turnip and Brie Soup

Carolyn Norberg, Soup Sister

Makes about 4 servings

2 Tbsp (30 mL) olive oil

1 onion, finely chopped

4 apples, peeled, cored and cut into ½-inch (1 cm) pieces

1 stalk celery, diced

2 Tbsp (30 mL) Cognac (optional)

3 cloves garlic, minced

6 cups (1.5 L) chicken or vegetable stock (approx.)

5 cups (1.25 L) ½-inch (1 cm) cubes peeled turnip

2 cups (500 mL) 1-inch (2.5 cm) cubes good-quality brie (without rind)

1 cup (250 mL) whipping cream (35% MF)

2 Tbsp (30 mL) maple syrup

Salt and pepper to taste

This was one of the first recipes I developed when I opened my business, Red House Soups, in St. John's. I wanted to create a soup that used turnips as they're one of our most abundant local vegetables. The soup has been popular with our customers ever since. You can even serve this soup as a dessert by topping each bowlful with 2 Tbsp (30 mL) candied pecans, a handful of blueberries and a drizzle of warm maple syrup.
—Carolyn Norberg

1. In a large pot, heat the oil over medium heat. Add the onion. Cook, stirring often, until the onion starts to soften.

2. Reduce the heat to low. Add the apples and celery. Cook, stirring often, until the onion has softened and the apples start to release their juice.

3. Add the Cognac (if using) and garlic. Cook, stirring, until the Cognac evaporates and garlic is cooked, about 1 minute.

4. Add 6 cups (1.5 L) stock and the turnip. Bring to a boil.

5. Reduce the heat and simmer, uncovered, until the turnip is tender, 20 to 30 minutes.

6. Remove the pot from the heat. Add the brie, cream and maple syrup.

7. Purée the soup until smooth. Reheat gently. If the soup seems too thick, add a little more warm stock. Season with salt and pepper to taste.

8. Ladle the soup into bowls and tuck in.

Barley, Red Bean and Spinach Soup

Ricardo Larrivée, Chef, TV Host (*Ricardo and Friends*) and Cookbook Author

Makes about 8 servings

Broth

1 Tbsp (15 mL) butter

4 ham hocks, rind removed

4 slices bacon, cut in half

10 cups (2.5 L) water

2 carrots, peeled and cut into chunks

2 stalks celery, cut into chunks

1 onion, quartered

1 tsp (5 mL) whole black peppercorns

2 bay leaves

Soup

2 Tbsp (30 mL) butter

1 leek (white part only), thinly sliced

2 cloves garlic, minced

2 carrots, peeled and thinly sliced

1 can (19 oz/540 mL) red kidney beans, drained and rinsed

½ cup (125 mL) pearl barley, rinsed and drained

Salt and pepper to taste

6 cups (1.5 L) lightly packed baby spinach

1. For the broth, heat the butter in a large pot over medium heat. Add the ham hocks and bacon. Cook, turning often, until the ham hocks and bacon are browned.

2. Add the water, carrots, celery, onion, peppercorns and bay leaves. Bring to a boil.

3. Reduce the heat and simmer, covered, until the ham hocks are tender, 1½ hours.

4. Remove the ham hocks from the pot and set aside to cool. When cool enough to handle, remove the meat from the hocks and shred it. Set aside.

5. Strain the broth through a fine-mesh sieve, discarding the vegetables and bacon. You will need 8 cups (2 L) of the broth for the soup. Add some extra water if there's too little or freeze the remainder if there's too much.

6. For the soup, heat the butter in the same large pot over medium heat. Add the leek and garlic. Cook, stirring often, until the leek has softened.

7. Add the reserved ham hock broth, carrots, beans, barley, and salt and pepper to taste. Bring to a boil, reduce the heat and simmer, covered, until the barley is tender, about 1 hour.

8. Stir in the spinach and reserved ham hock meat. Cook, stirring gently, until the spinach wilts. If the soup is too thick, add a little more ham hock broth (if any) or water. Season with salt and pepper to taste.

9. Ladle up hearty bowlfuls and enjoy.

Butternut Squash and Tomato Soup

Stephanie Sacks, Soup Sister

Makes about 4 servings

1 Tbsp (15 mL) olive oil
4 stalks celery, thinly sliced
3 shallots, thinly sliced
5 cups (1.25 L) peeled, seeded and cubed butternut squash (1 small squash)
3 cups (750 mL) water
1 can (14 oz/398 mL) diced tomatoes
½ tsp (2 mL) salt
½ tsp (2 mL) pepper

This recipe doubles—or even triples—well, and it freezes beautifully. To save time, I use my food processor to slice the celery and shallots, and buy packages of ready cubed squash.
—Stephanie Sacks

1. In a large pot, heat the oil over medium heat. Add the celery and shallots. Cook, stirring often, until the shallots are starting to soften but are not brown.

2. Add the squash, water, tomatoes, salt and pepper. Bring to a boil.

3. Reduce the heat and simmer, covered, until the squash is tender enough to mash with the back of a spoon, about 45 minutes.

4. Purée the soup until smooth. Reheat gently. Season with salt and pepper to taste.

5. Ladle up creamy bowlfuls and enjoy.

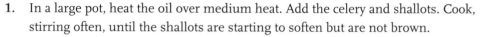

Caramelized Cauliflower Soup with Roasted Chanterelles

Jason Scharf, Broth Brother

Makes about 6 servings

Roasted Chanterelles and Corn

12 oz (375 g) chanterelle mushrooms, wiped clean

2 cups (500 mL) fresh corn kernels (see page 26)

2 Tbsp (30 mL) grapeseed oil, divided

2 shallots, minced and divided

2 cloves garlic, minced and divided

2 tsp (10 mL) finely chopped fresh thyme, divided

Salt and pepper to taste

Soup

1 Tbsp (15 mL) grapeseed oil

1 cauliflower, trimmed and divided into florets

Salt and pepper to taste

2 Tbsp (30 mL) butter

2 large shallots, finely chopped

4 cloves garlic, minced

½ cup (125 mL) white wine

5 cups (1 L) vegetable stock

2 cups (750 mL) whipping cream (35% MF)

½ cup (125 mL) finely chopped chives

½ cup (125 mL) finely chopped parsley

¼ cup (60 mL) finely chopped fresh dill

1 Tbsp (15 mL) crushed Marash chili (see sidebar) or 1 tsp (5 mL) red chili flakes

Extra virgin olive oil for garnish

Crushed Marash chilies have less heat and a fruitier flavor than regular red chili flakes. You can buy them online at silkroadspices.ca.

1. For the roasted chanterelles and corn, preheat the oven to 450°F (230°C).

2. Spread out the mushrooms and corn in separate small shallow roasting pans. To each pan add half of the oil, shallots, garlic and thyme, and salt and pepper to taste. Toss well.

cont'd on page 23

3. Roast until just barely crispy and golden, about 10 minutes. Remove from the oven and set aside.

4. For the soup, heat the oil in a large pot over medium-high heat.

5. In batches, sear the cauliflower until golden brown on all sides, sprinkling the cauliflower with salt and pepper to taste as it cooks and removing each batch to a plate once it's browned.

6. Return all the cauliflower to the pot. Reduce the heat to medium.

7. Add the butter, shallots and garlic. Cook, stirring often, until the shallots have softened.

8. Add the wine and bring to a boil, stirring to scrape up any browned bits from the bottom of the pot. Boil until the wine has almost all evaporated.

9. Add the stock. Bring to a boil.

10. Reduce the heat and simmer, covered, until the cauliflower is tender, 20 to 30 minutes.

11. Stir in the cream and bring back to a boil.

12. Purée the soup until smooth. Strain through a fine-mesh sieve back into the rinsed-out pot.

13. Reheat gently. Stir in the chives, parsley and dill, and salt and pepper to taste.

14. Ladle into soup bowls. Divide the roasted chanterelles and corn among the bowls, then garnish with Marash chili and a drizzle of olive oil.

When my Aunt Sharon (Hapton) asked me to come up with a soup recipe, I was inspired by a trip to the Calgary Farmers' Market and the amazing in-season vegetables on display there.
—Jason Scharf

Chili, Lime and Kale Soup with Aged White Cheddar

Patricia Green and Carolyn Hemming, Cookbook Authors

Makes about 4 servings

Full of fiber, antioxidants and valuable micronutrients, kale and quinoa make a power combination that not only tastes terrific, but is also great for detox and for cancer and disease prevention. The wonderful harmony of flavors in this soup is a result of the affinity kale has with lime zest and aged cheddar.
—Patricia Green and Carolyn Hemming

1 Tbsp (15 mL) grapeseed or vegetable oil

1 cup (250 mL) finely chopped onions

1½ tsp (7 mL) minced garlic

1 to 4 tsp (5 to 20 mL) minced, seeded serrano or jalapeño chili

4 cups (1 L) thinly sliced kale, center ribs and stems removed (1 large bunch)

4 cups (1 L) vegetable or chicken stock

1 cup (250 mL) water

½ cup (125 mL) quinoa

2 tsp (10 mL) finely grated lime zest

¼ tsp (1 mL) salt (optional)

⅓ cup (80 mL) shredded aged white cheddar cheese for garnish

1. In a large pot, heat the oil over medium-low heat. Stir in the onions. Cook, covered, until the onions start to soften. If the pot gets dry, add a few tablespoonfuls of water.

2. Add the garlic and chilies. Cook, stirring, for 1 minute.

3. Add the kale, stock, water and quinoa. Bring to a boil.

4. Reduce the heat and simmer, covered, until the quinoa is tender, 15 to 20 minutes.

5. Stir in the lime zest and salt (if using).

6. Ladle generously into soup bowls and top with a sprinkling of cheddar cheese.

This recipe is reprinted from Quinoa Revolution: Over 150 Recipes Under 500 Calories *by Patricia Green and Carolyn Hemming, 2012. Reprinted by permission of Penguin Books Canada Inc.*

Chorizo and Kale Soup

Caren McSherry, Cookbook Author and Owner, The Gourmet
Warehouse, Vancouver

Makes about 8 servings

⅓ cup (80 mL) olive oil
1 large onion, finely chopped
½ cup (125 mL) diced spicy pancetta
2 stalks celery, finely diced
1 large carrot, peeled and finely diced
2 large cloves garlic, minced
1 Tbsp (15 mL) chili paste (see sidebar)
1 large sprig sage
8 cups (2 L) chicken stock
4 cups (1 L) thinly sliced kale, center ribs
    and stems removed (1 large bunch)

1 can (19 oz/540 mL) white navy or
    cannellini beans, drained and rinsed
2 dry-cured chorizo sausages (each
    6 inches/15 cm), thinly sliced
½ cup (125 mL) finely chopped parsley
½ cup (125 mL) finely chopped cilantro
Salt and pepper to taste
⅔ cup (160 mL) freshly grated Parmesan
    cheese for garnish

*For best results, use
Côte d'Azur Spice 2.0
chili paste. It's spicy,
rich and fragrant,
with amazing depth
of flavor.*

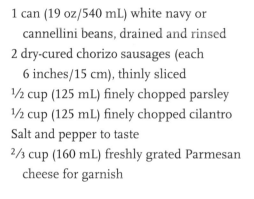

1. In a large pot, heat the oil over medium heat. Add the onion and cook, stirring often, until the onion has softened. Add the pancetta and cook, stirring often, until browned.

2. Add the celery, carrot, garlic, chili paste and sage. Cover and simmer for 10 minutes.

3. Add the stock, kale and beans, and bring to a boil.

4. Reduce the heat and simmer, covered, until the vegetables are tender, about 30 minutes.

5. Meanwhile, fry the chorizo sausage in a small skillet over medium-high heat until crisp. Drain on paper towels.

6. Remove the sage stem from the soup, and stir in the parsley and cilantro. Season with salt and pepper to taste.

7. Ladle up steaming bowlfuls and top with the fried chorizo and a generous sprinkling of Parmesan.

*On this side of the
Atlantic, we think
of kale as a new
superfood, but in
Europe it's been a
popular vegetable
forever: added to soups,
shredded in salads
and sautéed as a side
dish. Here I've paired
it with beans and
chorizo for a kick-butt
soup that delivers great
flavor and gets you
on the fast track to a
healthier you.*
—Caren McSherry

Crab and Corn Chowder with Bacon and Thyme

Michael Smith, Chef and Cookbook Author

The easiest way to remove the kernels from an ear of corn is to stand it on end in a large bowl. Hold the ear with one hand and, using a serrated knife, firmly slice off the kernels, allowing them to fall into the bowl, which will also contain any splatter.

This thick, rustic chowder is the first dish I make every year when our local corn comes into season. It's quite simply one of the very best ways to show off the sweetness of great corn—especially when you stir in lots of decadent crabmeat, crisp bacon and aromatic fresh thyme.
—Michael Smith

Makes about 4 servings

6 slices bacon, thinly sliced crosswise
1 large onion, finely chopped
2 stalks celery, diced
2 baking potatoes, peeled and diced
2 cups (500 mL) fresh corn kernels (about 2 ears)
2 cups (500 mL) chicken stock
2 cups (500 mL) whipping cream (35% MF)
8 oz (250 g) crabmeat
½ cup (125 mL) chopped parsley
1 Tbsp (15 mL) chopped fresh thyme
Salt and pepper to taste

1. In a large pot, cook the bacon over medium heat until it is lightly browned and crisp. Transfer to paper towels to drain.

2. Pour off all but a tablespoon or two (15 to 30 mL) of the bacon fat. Add the onion and celery to the pot and cook, stirring often, until the onion has softened.

3. Add the potatoes, corn, stock and cream and bring to a simmer.

4. Reduce the heat and simmer, uncovered and stirring occasionally, until the potatoes are tender, about 10 minutes.

5. Just before serving, pick over the crabmeat to remove any stray pieces of shell. Stir the crabmeat, parsley and thyme into the chowder. Simmer just long enough to heat everything through, about 2 minutes. Season with a little salt and lots of pepper.

6. Ladle the chowder into bowls and top with the reserved bacon. Serve and share!

Good-for-You Fish Chowder

Julie Daniluk, Soup Sister

Celeriac—aka celery root—is a brown, knobby vegetable. Peel off the skin and inside is white flesh, similar to rutabaga but with a celery flavor.

Job's tears (*yi yi ren*) is a tropical grass whose grain looks and tastes like barley but doesn't contain gluten. Look for it in Asian grocery stores, where it's often called Chinese pearl barley.

This soup is rich in ingredients with anti-inflammatory properties. Quinoa is rich in magnesium, which helps to relax blood vessels and thereby alleviate migraines. Spinach and mushrooms are a great source of folate (vitamin B9), and folate deficiency can contribute to atherosclerosis and dementia.
—Julie Daniluk

Makes about 8 servings

8 cups (2 L) vegetable stock
2 cups (500 mL) finely chopped leeks (white parts only) or onions
2 cups (500 mL) peeled and cubed celeriac (see sidebar) or turnip
1 cup (250 mL) Job's tears (see sidebar), soaked in water overnight and drained, or quinoa, rinsed and drained
1 cup (250 mL) sliced shiitake mushroom caps
2 Tbsp (30 mL) peeled and finely chopped fresh ginger
2 cloves garlic, minced
1 lb (500 g) boneless, skinless white fish (halibut, black cod or pollock)
6 cups (1.5 L) lightly packed baby spinach
1 cup (250 mL) finely chopped fresh basil or cilantro
1 cup (250 mL) unsweetened coconut milk
½ tsp (2 mL) pink rock or grey sea salt
Fresh lime juice to taste
1 tsp (5 mL) ground flaxseed (optional)
2 green onions, finely chopped, for garnish

1. In a large pot, combine the stock, leeks, celeriac, Job's tears, mushrooms, ginger and garlic. Bring to a rolling boil.

2. Reduce the heat and simmer, covered, for 45 minutes.

3. Place the fish on top of the ingredients. Simmer, covered, until the fish flakes with a fork, about 15 minutes.

4. Gently stir in the spinach, basil, coconut milk and salt. Simmer for 5 minutes. Season with lime juice to taste. If using quinoa, add the flaxseed to thicken the soup slightly.

5. Ladle the soup into bowls and add a scattering of green onions to each.

Grilled Corn and Clam Chowder

David Robertson, Chef/Owner, The Dirty Apron Cooking School and Delicatessen, Vancouver

Makes about 4 servings

40 fresh manila clams in their shells, scrubbed

1 cup (250 mL) white wine

2 ears of corn, shucked

8 oz (250 g) double-smoked bacon, cut into
½-inch (1 cm) pieces

4 shallots, finely chopped

1 small carrot, peeled and diced

4 cloves garlic, minced

2 cups (500 mL) bottled clam juice or nectar

4 small unpeeled red-skinned potatoes
(8 oz/250 g), diced

2 Tbsp (30 mL) cold water

2 tsp (10 mL) cornstarch

1 cup (250 mL) whipping cream (35% MF)

3 Tbsp (45 mL) fresh lemon juice

2 tsp (10 mL) finely chopped fresh thyme

Salt and pepper to taste

2 tsp (10 mL) finely chopped chives for garnish

1. Discard any clams that don't close when tapped sharply on the counter.

2. In a medium saucepan, bring the wine to a boil over medium-high heat. Add the clams. Cover and steam until the clams open, 6 to 8 minutes. Discard any clams that don't open.

3. Remove the clams from the saucepan, reserving the cooking liquid. Remove the meat from the clam shells, discarding the shells. Refrigerate the clam meat. Strain the cooking liquid through a fine-mesh sieve into a medium bowl and set aside.

4. Preheat the barbecue to medium-high. Grill the corn, turning often, until golden brown, about 5 minutes (corn won't be tender). Using a sharp knife, cut the kernels off the ears and set aside.

5. In a large pot, cook the bacon over medium heat until browned and crisp, about 5 minutes. Drain on paper towels.

6. Pour off all but 1 Tbsp (15 mL) of the bacon fat. Add the shallots, carrot and garlic to the pot and cook, stirring often, until the shallots have softened.

7. Add the clam juice, potatoes and reserved clam cooking liquid to the saucepan. Bring to a boil. Reduce the heat and simmer, covered, for 10 minutes.

8. In a small bowl, stir together the water and cornstarch until smooth. Add the cornstarch mixture to the soup, along with the corn kernels, reserved clam meat and bacon, cream, lemon juice and thyme. Bring to a boil.

9. Reduce the heat and simmer, uncovered, until the potatoes and corn are tender, about 5 minutes. Season with salt and pepper to taste.

10. Ladle the chowder into bowls and garnish with a scattering of chives.

Green Split Pea Soup with Fennel

Marion Schell, Soup Sister

Makes about 6 servings

2 Tbsp (30 mL) olive oil
1 cup (250 mL) finely chopped onions
2 cups (500 mL) diced fennel with tops
1 cup (250 mL) peeled and diced carrots
1 cup (250 mL) diced celery
8 cups (2 L) water
2 cups (500 mL) green split peas, picked over and rinsed
1 ham bone
Salt and pepper to taste
Parsley for garnish

1. In a large pot, heat the oil over medium heat. Add the onions. Cook, stirring often, until the onions have softened.

2. Add the fennel, carrots and celery. Cook, stirring often, for 2 minutes.

3. Add the water, split peas and ham bone. Bring to a boil.

4. Reduce the heat and simmer, covered, until the split peas are tender, 1½ to 2 hours.

5. Remove the ham bone. Season with salt and pepper to taste.

6. Ladle the soup into bowls, garnish with parsley and get cozy.

The aromas wafting from this ham bone–based stock scream for wool socks and a flannel nightie. Cuddle up by the fire with a bowl of this old-fashioned soup and a thick slice of homemade bread slathered with butter.
—Marion Schell

Israeli Orange Vegetable Soup with Zhoug

Bonnie Stern, Cookbook Author and Food Columnist

Makes about 6 servings

Orange soup—the color, not the flavor—is very popular in Israel because so many people are vegetarian. Make this soup with one orange vegetable or lots of them. I even add matzo balls at Jewish celebration dinners for my vegetarian guests. A splash of bright-green zhoug (a spicy cilantro pesto) adds another layer of flavor or, if you prefer, add a swirl of sour cream or yogurt, or crumbled feta or soft goat cheese. You can even add 1 tsp (5 mL) ground cumin or sweet smoked paprika or 1 Tbsp (15 mL) curry paste with the onions. It's all about making the recipe your own.
—Bonnie Stern

2 Tbsp (30 mL) olive oil
1 onion, finely chopped
2 cloves garlic, minced
1 lb (500 g) butternut squash, peeled, seeded and diced (2 cups/500 mL)
1 lb (500 g) sweet potatoes, peeled and diced (2 cups/500 mL)
1 lb (500 g) carrots, peeled and diced (2 cups/500 mL)
Salt and pepper to taste
4 cups (1 L) vegetable stock or water (approx.)

Zhoug

2 cloves garlic, peeled
½ jalapeño chili, coarsely chopped (less if it's very hot)
1 bunch cilantro, roots and tough stems removed
½ tsp (2 mL) salt
½ cup (125 mL) extra virgin olive oil

1. For the soup, heat the oil over medium heat in a large pot. Add the onion and garlic. Cook, stirring often, until the onion has softened but is not brown.

2. Add the squash, sweet potatoes, carrots, and salt and pepper to taste. Cook, stirring often, for 3 minutes.

3. Add the stock and bring to a boil.

4. Reduce the heat and simmer, covered, until the vegetables are very tender, about 30 minutes.

5. Purée the soup until smooth. If the soup is too thick, add a little more stock or water so that it is the consistency of heavy cream or whatever consistency you like.

6. For the zhoug, chop the garlic and jalapeño in a food processor or mini chopper. Add the cilantro and salt. Process until finely chopped. Drizzle in the oil and process until well combined. Season with more salt to taste.

7. Reheat the soup gently. Season with salt and pepper to taste.

8. Ladle into wide soup bowls and serve drizzled with a colorful swirl of zhoug.

Lentil, Kale and Sausage Soup

Claire Tansey, Food Director, *Chatelaine*

Makes about 6 servings

2 Tbsp (30 mL) olive oil
2 hot or sweet Italian sausages
1 large onion, finely chopped
1 leek (white part only), thinly sliced
3 carrots, peeled and diced
2 cloves garlic, minced
1 can (5½ oz/156 mL) tomato paste
1 tsp (5 mL) ground coriander
1 tsp (5 mL) salt
4 cups (1 L) water
8 cups (2 L) chopped kale, center ribs and stems removed (about 1 small bunch)
1 can (19 oz/540 mL) lentils, drained and rinsed
Freshly grated Parmesan cheese for garnish (optional)

1. Heat a large pot over medium heat. Add the oil, then the sausages. Cook the sausages, turning occasionally, until the outsides lose their pink color, 4 to 6 minutes (the sausages won't be completely cooked). Transfer the sausages to a plate.

2. Add the onion, leek, carrots and garlic to the pot. Cook, stirring often, until the onion starts to soften.

3. Thinly slice the sausages. Add the sausages and any of their juices to the saucepan, along with the tomato paste, coriander and salt. Cook, stirring often, for 5 minutes.

4. Add the water and bring to a boil. Stir in the kale.

5. Reduce the heat and simmer, covered and stirring occasionally, until the sausage is cooked and the kale is just tender, 5 to 7 minutes.

6. Stir in the lentils and heat through. If the soup is too thick, stir in a little more water.

7. Ladle into soup bowls and sprinkle generously with Parmesan (if using).

Lobster Cappuccino

Matt Dean Pettit, Chef/Owner, Rock Lobster Food Co., Toronto, and Cookbook Author

Makes about 6 servings

8 cups (2 L) water
1 Tbsp (15 mL) salt
2 live lobsters (each 1½ lb/750 g)
2 Tbsp (30 mL) olive oil
1 cup (250 mL) diced fennel
1 cup (250 mL) peeled and diced carrots
1 cup (250 mL) peeled, seeded and diced tomatoes
½ cup (125 mL) finely chopped shallots

¼ cup (60 mL) butter
1 Tbsp (15 mL) tomato paste
2 cups (500 mL) white wine
3 cups (750 mL) chicken stock
½ cup (125 mL) whipping cream (35% MF)
Crème fraîche for garnish (see page 182)
Finely chopped chives for garnish

1. Bring the water to a boil in a large pot. Add the salt, then the lobsters, head first. Boil for 10 to 12 minutes.

2. Have ready a sink full of ice water. Remove the lobsters from the pot, reserving the cooking water, and plunge the lobsters into the ice water. When cool enough to handle, shell the lobsters (see sidebar), reserving the shells.

3. Coarsely chop the lobster meat, then cover and refrigerate it.

4. In a large pot, heat the oil over medium-high heat. Add the lobster shells. Cook, stirring often, to release the flavors, about 5 minutes.

5. Add the fennel, carrots, tomatoes, shallots, butter and tomato paste. Reduce the heat to medium and cook, stirring often, until the shallots have softened.

6. Add the wine and bring to a boil, stirring any browned bits from the bottom of the pot.

7. Add the stock and reserved lobster cooking water. Bring to a boil, then reduce the heat and simmer, covered, for about 1 hour.

8. Strain through a fine-mesh sieve into a clean pot. Be careful as the soup will be very hot; it's easier to do this with a helper. If necessary, strain again to make sure all the vegetables and shells are removed.

9. Add the cream to the soup and heat through over medium heat.

10. Ladle the bisque into bowls. Spoon a dollop of crème fraîche into each portion. Top with the reserved lobster meat and finish with a scattering of chopped chives.

Lobster 101
To shell a lobster, first twist off its legs. With a hammer or the side of a large, heavy knife, smack the lobster claws until they crack in several places. With a lobster pick or wooden skewer, remove the meat from the legs, claws and knuckles. Cut the tails open with scissors and remove the meat.

In the fall of 2012, I was part of a great charity event called Soupstock. More than 200 chefs from Canada and the U.S. gathered to make and sell soup to raise money to fight a proposed mega-quarry slated for agricultural land. More than 40,000 people came out to support the charity that day and I served 3,500 portions of this soup!
—Matt Dean Pettit

Mama Palacz's Chicken and Vegetable Soup with Dill

Erin Barr, Soup Sister

Makes about 6 servings

2 Tbsp (30 mL) olive oil

1 onion, finely chopped

5 carrots, peeled and diced

5 stalks celery, diced

8 cups (2 L) chicken or vegetable stock or water

2 cups (500 mL) peeled and cubed white or sweet potatoes

2 cups (500 mL) chopped green beans (fresh or frozen)

4 boneless, skinless chicken breasts, cut into bite-size pieces

1 large bunch fresh dill, coarsely chopped

Salt and pepper to taste

I first had this soup when staying with friends at a cabin in Sicamous, B.C., where my friend's mom (the Mama Palacz of the title) had made it. I loved the fresh flavors so decided to come up with my own version. It's good any time of year.
—Erin Barr

1. In a large pot, heat the oil over medium heat. Add the onion. Cook, stirring often, until the onion has softened.

2. Add the carrots and celery. Cook, stirring often, for 5 minutes.

3. Add the stock, potatoes and green beans. Bring to a boil.

4. Reduce the heat and simmer, covered, for 5 minutes.

5. Add the chicken. Simmer, covered, until the chicken is no longer pink inside and the vegetables are tender, about 15 minutes.

6. Add the dill. Season with salt and pepper to taste.

7. Ladle the soup into bowls and dig in.

Most Excellent Red Lentil Soup

Susan Schwartz, Soup Sister

Makes about 8 servings

3 to 4 Tbsp (45 to 60 mL) olive oil

½ tsp (2 mL) curry powder

½ tsp (2 mL) ground cumin

½ tsp (2 mL) red chili flakes

½ tsp (2 mL) dried thyme leaves

2 large onions, finely chopped

1 piece (2- x 1-inch/5 x 2.5 cm) fresh ginger, peeled and minced

4 cloves garlic, minced

2 cups (500 mL) red lentils, picked over and rinsed

4 stalks celery, finely diced

3 carrots, peeled and finely diced

4 cups (1 L) water

4 cups (1 L) chicken or vegetable stock

1 can (28 oz/796 mL) diced tomatoes or 3 cups (750 mL) coarsely chopped fresh tomatoes

2 Tbsp (30 mL) ketchup

2 tsp (10 mL) maple syrup or brown sugar

1 tsp (5 mL) salt

½ tsp (2 mL) pepper

2 bay leaves

½ cup (125 mL) sherry (optional)

If made with vegetable stock, this soup is vegetarian. It can be vegan, too, depending on the brand of ketchup, and if maple syrup is used instead of sugar (bone char is used in the processing of some cane sugars).

1. In a large pot, heat the oil over medium heat. Add the curry powder, cumin, chili flakes and thyme. Cook, stirring often, until the spices are fragrant, 1 to 2 minutes.

2. Add the onions. Cook, stirring often, until the onions have softened.

3. Add the ginger and garlic. Cook, stirring, until fragrant, about 1 minute.

4. Add the lentils, celery and carrots. Cook, stirring often, until the vegetables start to soften, about 15 minutes.

5. Add the water, stock, tomatoes, ketchup, maple syrup, salt, pepper and bay leaves. Bring to a boil.

6. Reduce the heat and simmer, covered, until the vegetables and lentils are very tender, about 1½ hours.

7. Remove the bay leaves. Add the sherry (if using). If you like, blend the soup slightly with an immersion blender in the pot. Season with salt and pepper to taste.

8. Ladle up hearty bowlfuls and enjoy.

This recipe came to me from Gerry Korda, whose daughter is married to my youngest son. I tweaked it slightly, adding fresh ginger and cumin, but either ingredient—or both— can be omitted. Both of us have cooked this soup in considerably larger quantities in the Meals on Wheels kitchen at Congregation Shaar Hashomayim in Westmount, Quebec, where we volunteer. And it's a cold-weather favorite in our homes, too.
—Susan Schwartz

Pear, Parsnip and Celeriac Soup with Pumpkin Seed Salsa Verde

Jonathan Chovancek, Chef/Co-owner, Bittered Sling Extracts and Bittered Sling Bistro, Vancouver

Makes about 6 servings

Pumpkin Seed Salsa Verde

¼ cup (60 mL) roasted unsalted pumpkin seeds

1 jalapeño chili, seeded and thinly sliced

1 clove garlic, peeled

½ bunch cilantro, roots and tough stems removed

12 fresh mint leaves

Finely grated zest of 1 lemon

¼ cup (60 mL) cold-pressed sunflower seed oil

Fresh lemon juice to taste

Salt and pepper to taste

Soup

10 to 12 parsnips, scrubbed (not peeled), trimmed and diced

1 large head celeriac (see page 28), peeled and diced

¼ cup (60 mL) cold-pressed sunflower seed oil, divided

Salt and pepper to taste

1 small onion, finely chopped

2 cloves garlic, thinly sliced

6 ripe pears, peeled, cored and diced

2 white potatoes, peeled and diced

1 bay leaf

4 cups (1 L) water or chicken stock

Fresh lemon juice to taste

1. For the salsa verde, use a mortar and pestle to grind the pumpkin seeds, jalapeño and garlic to a coarse paste. Add the cilantro, mint and lemon zest. Continue grinding to form a coarse paste.

2. Grind in the oil, lemon juice, and salt and pepper to taste. Use a spatula to scoop the paste into an airtight container. (The salsa verde can be stored in the fridge to up to 5 days.)

3. For the soup, heat the oven to 375°F (190°C). In a shallow roasting pan, toss the parsnips, celeriac, 2 Tbsp (30 mL) of the oil, and salt and pepper to taste. Roast, uncovered and stirring, until the parsnips and celeriac are golden and tender, 30 to 40 minutes. Remove from the oven and set aside.

4. In a large pot, heat the remaining oil over medium heat. Add the onion and salt and pepper to taste. Cook, stirring often, until the onion has softened. Add the garlic. Cook, stirring, for 1 minute.

5. Add the pears, potatoes and bay leaf. Cook, stirring often, until the pears start to soften.

6. Add the roasted parsnips and celeriac and water. Bring to a boil, then reduce the heat and simmer, covered, until the vegetables are very tender, 30 to 40 minutes. Remove the bay leaf.

7. Purée the soup until smooth. Reheat gently. Season with lemon juice and salt and pepper to taste.

8. Ladle into bowls and add one or two teaspoonfuls (5 or 10 mL) of salsa verde to each bowl.

Pistou (Provençal Vegetable Soup)

Patricia Wells, Journalist, Cookbook Author and Cooking School Teacher

Makes about 8 servings

1 lb (500 g) fresh white (navy) beans in their
    pods or ½ cup (125 mL) dried navy beans (see
    page 4)

7 large garlic cloves, divided

¼ cup (60 mL) olive oil

1 bouquet garni (see sidebar)

Salt to taste

1½ lb (750 g) pumpkin, peeled, seeded and cubed

2 medium potatoes, peeled and cubed

2 large carrots, scrubbed (not peeled), quartered
    lengthwise and sliced

2 leeks (white parts only), quartered lengthwise
    and thinly sliced

1 onion, halved and thinly sliced into rings

12 cups (3 L) cold water (approx.)

8 oz (250 g) green beans, trimmed at both ends
    and cut crosswise into quarters

1 zucchini, quartered lengthwise and sliced

1 tomato, cored, peeled, seeded and chopped

1 Tbsp (15 mL) tomato paste

¼ cup (60 mL) very fine pasta, such as angel-hair

½ cup (125 mL) freshly grated Parmesan cheese

1. If using fresh beans, shell them and set aside. If using dried beans, soak and drain them (see page 4).

2. Peel the garlic. Cut 2 cloves in half lengthwise and set aside. Cut the remaining cloves in quarters lengthwise and set aside.

3. In a large, heavy-bottomed pot over medium heat, combine the oil, halved garlic cloves, bouquet garni and salt to taste, stirring to coat everything with the oil.

4. Cook, stirring often, until the garlic is soft but not colored, about 5 minutes.

5. Add the navy beans and stir to coat with the oil. Cook, stirring, for 1 minute.

6. Add the pumpkin, potatoes, carrots, leeks, onion and quartered garlic. Cook, stirring often, until the vegetables start to soften, about 10 minutes.

7. Add 12 cups (3 L) water, green beans, zucchini, tomato and tomato paste. Cover, bring to a boil, and boil for 7 minutes.

8. Reduce the heat and simmer, covered, until the navy beans are tender, about 30 minutes, adding more water if the soup becomes too thick.

9. Add the pasta and simmer, uncovered and stirring often to keep the pasta from sticking to the bottom of the pot, until the pasta is tender, about 5 minutes. Remove the bouquet garni and season with salt to taste.

10. Ladle up steaming bowlfuls and swirl Parmesan into each portion.

To make a bouquet garni, wrap several bay leaves and sprigs of thyme in a couple of layers of the green part of a leek, then tie securely with kitchen string.

    This traditional French vegetable soup can be vegan if you omit the cheese and use pasta that doesn't contain eggs, and can be gluten free if you use gluten-free pasta.

Potato-Cheddar Soup

Lynn Crawford, Chef/Owner of Ruby Watchco, Toronto, Cookbook Author and TV Host, *Pitchin' In*

Makes about 6 servings

¼ cup (60 mL) butter
2 lb (1 kg) russet potatoes, peeled and diced
2 carrots, peeled and diced
2 stalks celery, diced
1 large onion, finely chopped
1 leek (white part only), diced
Salt and pepper to taste
4 cups (1 L) chicken stock
1 cup (250 mL) whipping cream (35% MF)
1 cup (250 mL) shredded cheddar cheese
3 Tbsp (45 mL) finely chopped fresh dill

1. In a large, heavy-bottomed pot, melt the butter over medium heat. Add the potatoes, carrots, celery, onion, leek, and salt and pepper to taste. Cook, stirring often, until the vegetables are beginning to brown and the onion has softened.

2. Add the stock and bring to a boil over high heat.

3. Reduce the heat and simmer, covered, until the vegetables are tender, about 20 minutes.

4. Purée half of the soup until smooth.

5. Add the puréed soup back to the pot. Stir in the cream. Reheat gently.

6. Remove the pot from the heat. Stir in the cheese and dill and season with salt and pepper to taste. Ladle up brimming bowlfuls.

Red Lentil and Bottle Gourd Dal

Suki Kaur-Cosier, Owner, Cooking Matters Cooking School, London, Ontario

Makes about 4 servings

2 cups (500 mL) red lentils
8 cups (2 L) water
3 cups (750 mL) peeled and finely chopped bottle gourd (see sidebar)
1 tsp (5 mL) turmeric
Salt to taste
2 Tbsp (30 mL) vegetable oil
1 onion, finely chopped
1 Tbsp (15 mL) minced garlic
1 Tbsp (15 mL) peeled and grated fresh ginger
1 ripe tomato, finely chopped
1 tsp (5 mL) garam masala
Pinch of red chili flakes (or to taste)
Sour cream for garnish
Cilantro leaves for garnish

Bottle gourd, also called long green squash, looks like a cross between a cucumber and a zucchini. It has soft white flesh and edible seeds.

1. Wash the lentils in several changes of water.

2. In large, heavy-bottomed pot, combine the lentils, 8 cups (2 L) water, bottle gourd, turmeric and salt to taste. Bring to a boil.

3. Reduce the heat and simmer, covered, until the lentils are tender and the water has reduced a little, 20 to 30 minutes.

4. Meanwhile, in a small skillet, heat the oil over medium heat. Add the onion. Cook, stirring often, until the onion has softened.

5. Add the garlic and ginger. Cook, stirring often, until golden brown.

6. Add the tomato. Cook, stirring often, until the tomato has softened, about 5 minutes. Stir in the garam masala and chili flakes.

7. Add the onion mixture to the lentils and stir. If the soup seems too thick, add a little water and heat gently.

8. Ladle into bowls and garnish with a flourish of sour cream and a scattering of cilantro leaves.

Simple Butternut Squash Soup

Karen Miller, Soup Sister

Makes about 4 servings

2 Tbsp (30 mL) vegetable oil

1 small onion, finely chopped

1 butternut squash, peeled, seeded and cubed (about 5 cups/1.25 L)

2 Tbsp (30 mL) maple syrup

1 tsp (5 mL) salt

2 to 3 sprigs thyme

¼ tsp (1 mL) mild, medium or hot curry powder

¼ tsp (1 mL) ground cinnamon

Water as required (see method)

½ lemon

1. In a large pot, heat the oil over medium heat. Add the onion. Cook, stirring often, until the onion has softened.

2. Add the squash, maple syrup, salt, thyme sprigs, curry powder and cinnamon to the pot. Cook, stirring often, for 5 minutes.

3. Add enough water to cover the squash. Bring to a boil.

4. Reduce the heat and simmer, covered, until the squash is tender, about 20 minutes. Remove the thyme stems.

5. Purée the soup until smooth. Reheat gently. Add a squeeze of lemon juice.

6. Ladle up piping hot bowlfuls and dig in.

It may be simple to prepare, but this soup is silky in texture and luxurious in taste. It's the one most often requested by my friends and family, and is always satisfying for lunch or dinner. Add more spices if you like, but I think plain and simple is the best.
—Karen Miller

Spanish Chorizo and Chickpea Soup with Crostini

Curtis Stone, Chef and Cookbook Author

Makes about 4 servings

3 Tbsp (45 mL) olive oil, divided

6 oz (175 g) dry-cured Spanish chorizo sausage, casing removed, halved lengthwise and thinly sliced

1 onion, finely chopped

2 carrots, peeled and cut into ½-inch (1 cm) pieces

2 stalks celery, cut into ½-inch (1 cm) pieces

2 small fennel bulbs, cut into ½-inch (1 cm) pieces (about 2 cups/500 mL)

4 cloves garlic, minced

2 large sprigs thyme

1 sprig rosemary

¾ cup (185 mL) dry white wine

6 cups (1.5 L) chicken stock

Salt and pepper to taste

3 cups (750 mL) chickpeas (from two 19 oz/540 mL cans), drained

½ demi-baguette, cut diagonally into ½-inch (1 cm) slices

Extra virgin olive oil for garnish

1. In a large pot, heat 1 Tbsp (15 mL) of the oil over medium heat. Add the chorizo. Cook, stirring often, until browned.

2. Add the onion. Cook, stirring often, until the onion has softened.

3. Add the carrots, celery, fennel, garlic, thyme and rosemary. Cook, stirring often, until the vegetables start to soften.

4. Add the wine and bring to a simmer. Stir in the stock and season with salt and pepper to taste. Bring to a simmer.

5. Reduce the heat and simmer, uncovered, until the vegetables are tender, about 20 minutes.

6. Stir in the chickpeas and simmer gently to blend the flavors, about 10 minutes.

7. Remove the thyme and rosemary stems.

8. Meanwhile, brush the baguette slices with the remaining oil and sprinkle with salt. Toast in a toaster oven or under the broiler until golden brown on both sides.

9. Ladle the soup into soup bowls. Add a swirl of extra virgin olive oil to each and serve with the crostini.

Spiced Dal and Carrot Soup

Daniel Trottier, Executive Chef, Académie Culinaire, Montreal

Makes about 4 servings

½ cup (125 mL) red lentils, picked over and rinsed

3 cups (750 mL) chicken or vegetable stock

2 cups (500 mL) peeled and diced carrots

1½ cups (375 mL) canned crushed tomatoes

1 onion, finely chopped

1 garlic clove, minced

4 tsp (20 mL) ghee (see sidebar) or vegetable oil

½ tsp (2 mL) ground cumin

½ tsp (2 mL) ground coriander

½ tsp (2 mL) turmeric

Juice of ½ lemon

Salt and pepper to taste

⅔ cup (160 mL) whipping cream (35% MF)

For the smoothest, most velvety texture, use a blender (not a food processor or immersion blender) to purée this soup. Add the soup to the blender in batches, blending each batch for at least 4 minutes before straining it.

Ghee is a type of clarified butter that's used in South Asian cuisine. Look for it in Indian grocery stores.

1. In a large pot, combine the lentils, stock, carrots, tomatoes, onion and garlic. Bring to a boil.

2. Reduce the heat and simmer, covered, until the carrots are very tender, about 30 minutes.

3. Meanwhile, heat the ghee in a small skillet over medium heat. Add the cumin, coriander and turmeric. Cook, stirring, for 1 minute to develop the flavors.

4. Remove the skillet from the heat and add the lemon juice. Set aside.

5. Purée the soup until smooth (see sidebar). Strain through a fine-mesh sieve back into the rinsed-out pot.

6. Bring the soup to a simmer and add the spice mixture, a little at a time until you like the taste. Simmer for 10 minutes. Season with salt and pepper to taste. Stir in the cream.

7. Ladle up hearty bowlfuls.

Spicy Black Bean Soup with Smoky Chipotle and Roasted Peppers

Stuart Fleming, Innovation and Product Development Manager, Happy Planet Foods, Burnaby, B.C.

Makes about 6 servings

5 cups (1.25 L) water (approx.)

2 cups (500 mL) dried black beans, picked over and rinsed

1/8 tsp (0.5 mL) baking soda

2 bay leaves

1 tsp (5 mL) table salt

2 Tbsp (30 mL) olive oil

2 large onions, finely chopped

2 large stalks celery, diced

1 large carrot, peeled and diced

1 tsp (5 mL) sea salt

5 cloves garlic, minced

1 Tbsp (15 mL) ground cumin

1/2 tsp (2 mL) red chili flakes

3 cups (750 mL) vegetable stock

1 can (14 oz/398 mL) diced tomatoes

1 sweet red pepper, roasted (see page 179) and cut into 1-inch (2.5 cm) pieces

1 sweet green pepper, roasted (see page 179) and cut into 1-inch (2.5 cm) pieces

1/2 cup (125 mL) fresh corn kernels (see page 26)

1 Tbsp (15 mL) tomato paste

1 Tbsp (15 mL) minced canned chipotle chilies in adobo sauce (see page 49)

2 tsp (10 mL) adobo sauce (from can of chipotle chilies)

1 small bunch cilantro, roots and tough stems removed, divided

1 Tbsp (15 mL) fresh lime juice

Toppings (optional)

Finely chopped red onion

Sour cream

Lime wedges

Additional adobo sauce

cont'd on page 48

1. In a large saucepan, combine 5 cups (1.25 L) water, beans, baking soda and bay leaves. Bring to a boil. Add the table salt.

2. Reduce the heat and simmer, covered, until the beans are tender, 1 to 1½ hours, adding more water, if necessary, to keep the beans just submerged. (Dried beans can sometimes cook unevenly, so test several beans to ensure that they're completely tender.)

3. Don't drain the beans but remove the bay leaves. Set aside.

4. In a large pot, heat the oil over medium-high heat. Add the onions, celery, carrot and sea salt. Cook, stirring often, until the vegetables have softened and are beginning to brown.

5. Reduce the heat to medium. Add the garlic, cumin and chili flakes. Cook, stirring often, until fragrant, about 2 minutes.

6. Add the beans with their cooking liquid, the stock, tomatoes, roasted red and green peppers, corn, tomato paste, chipotle chilies and adobo sauce. Bring to a boil.

7. Reduce the heat and simmer, uncovered, for 30 minutes.

8. Finely chop half of the cilantro and add it to the soup. Tear the remaining cilantro into sprigs and set aside for garnish.

9. Add the lime juice to the soup. Season with more salt to taste.

10. Put the remaining cilantro and the other toppings (if using) in individual bowls.

11. Ladle the soup into soup bowls and serve with the toppings so everyone can help themselves.

This delicious, hearty soup is inspired by the rich flavors of Mexico and the southwest United States. The perfect combination of savory, sweet and spicy notes has made it a real favorite with all of us at Happy Planet Foods in Burnaby, B.C., and makes our team long for winter, when we can cook up a batch.
—Stuart Fleming

Sweet Potato and Chipotle Soup

Jeannine Scott, Owner, Soupe Café, Montreal

Makes about 4 servings

2 lb (1 kg) sweet potatoes, scrubbed (not peeled)
6 cups (1.5 L) chicken or vegetable stock
⅓ cup (80 mL) tomato sauce
3 Tbsp (45 mL) butter
2 Tbsp (30 mL) 2% milk
½ tsp (2 mL) dried thyme leaves
Pepper to taste
1 to 2 tsp (5 to 10 mL) minced canned chipotle chilies in adobo sauce (according to taste; see sidebar)
Chopped cashews for garnish

1. Preheat the oven to 375°F (190°C).
2. Cut the sweet potatoes in half and place cut sides down on a large baking sheet. Bake until tender, about 1 hour.
3. Remove the sweet potatoes from the oven and, when cool enough to handle, peel away and discard the skin.
4. In a medium bowl, mash the sweet potatoes. (They don't have to be completely smooth.)
5. In a large pot, combine the mashed sweet potatoes, chicken stock, tomato sauce, butter, milk, thyme and pepper to taste. Bring to a boil.
6. Reduce the heat and simmer, covered, for 45 minutes. Stir in the chipotle chilies.
7. Purée the soup until smooth. Reheat gently.
8. Ladle into bowls and add a topping of crunchy cashews to each.

Chipotle chilies are smoked jalapeños that are canned in spicy adobo sauce. Look for them in the Mexican section of larger grocery stores. Scrape the remainder of the can into a small freezer bag and freeze for several months. Use straight from the freezer whenever you want to add a touch of smoky spice to a recipe.

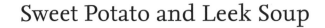
vegan   gluten free

Sweet Potato and Leek Soup

Miriam Bronstein, Soup Sister

Makes about 6 servings

1 Tbsp (15 mL) canola oil
2 cups (500 mL) chopped leeks (white parts only)
2 carrots, peeled and diced
1 onion, finely chopped
2 cloves garlic, minced
4 cups (1 L) peeled and coarsely chopped sweet potatoes
4 cups (1 L) water
½ cup (125 mL) white wine
¼ cup (60 mL) finely chopped parsley
½ tsp (2 mL) salt
½ tsp (2 mL) white pepper
¼ cup (60 mL) finely chopped chives or green onions for garnish

1. In a large pot, heat the oil over medium heat. Add the leeks, carrots, onion and garlic. Cook, stirring often, until the onion has softened.

2. Add the sweet potatoes, water and wine. Bring to a boil.

3. Reduce the heat. Add the parsley, salt and pepper. Simmer, covered, until the vegetables are tender, 25 to 30 minutes.

4. Purée the soup until smooth. Reheat gently. Season with more salt and pepper to taste.

5. Ladle up golden bowlfuls and sprinkle with chives.

Swiss Chard, Sausage and Parmesan Soup

Andrea Nicholson, Chef/Owner, Killer Condiments, Toronto

Makes about 6 servings

1 lb (500 g) sweet or hot Italian sausages

2 Tbsp (30 mL) olive oil

1 onion, finely chopped

3 cloves garlic, minced

1 tsp (5 mL) sea salt

½ tsp (2 mL) dried Italian herb seasoning

½ tsp (2 mL) pepper

¼ tsp (1 mL) red chili flakes

1 cup (250 mL) white wine

4 cups (1 L) chicken stock

3 cups (750 mL) peeled and diced Yukon Gold potatoes

1 cup (250 mL) canned diced tomatoes with their juice

2 cups (500 mL) well-packed coarsely chopped Swiss chard leaves or other hearty green

½ cup (125 mL) shaved Parmesan cheese

Never throw away your Parmesan cheese rind—it makes a great flavor enhancer if you add it to a pot of simmering soup. Just don't forget to remove it before serving.

1. Remove the sausages from their casings and cut them into 1-inch (2.5 cm) pieces.

2. In a large pot, heat the oil over medium-high heat. Add the sausage. Cook, stirring often, until the sausage is browned. (The sausage won't be completely cooked.) Transfer to a bowl. Drain the excess fat from the pot.

3. Add the onion, garlic, salt, herb seasoning, pepper and chili flakes to the pot. Cook, stirring often, until the onion is starting to soften.

4. Add the wine and bring to a boil, stirring to scrape up any browned bits from the bottom of the pot. Let the wine bubble for 2 to 4 minutes.

5. Add the stock, potatoes and tomatoes. Bring to a boil and return the sausage to the pot.

6. Reduce the heat and simmer, covered, until the potatoes are almost tender, about 10 minutes.

7. Add the Swiss chard and simmer, covered, until tender, about 5 minutes.

8. Season with salt and pepper to taste. Ladle into soup bowls and scatter with shaved Parmesan.

I love making hearty soups like this that are full of flavor, substantial and easily adaptable. I often change up the vegetables with whatever is in my fridge, or even leave out the sausage and use vegetable stock to make it vegetarian. Serve with warm, buttery bread.
—Andrea Nicholson

Tomato and Peanut Soup with Sweet Potato and Chickpeas

Julie Van Rosendaal, Cookbook Author and Blogger, dinnerwithjulie.com

Makes about 8 servings

This versatile soup can be made on the stovetop or in a slow cooker. Hearty and rich, it gets a boost of protein from the peanut butter and chickpeas. To make it a more substantial meal, serve over a shallow bowl of rice. In fact, with a spoonful of curry paste or powder added along with the spices, and less stock (or use coconut milk instead), it makes a delicious curry.
—Julie Van Rosendaal

1 Tbsp (15 mL) vegetable oil (optional)

1 onion, finely chopped

2 Tbsp (30 mL) peeled and grated fresh ginger

3 cloves garlic, minced

1 to 2 jalapeño chilies, seeded and finely chopped

2 tsp (10 mL) chili powder

1½ tsp (7 mL) ground cumin

1 tsp (5 mL) salt

4 cups (1 L) chicken or vegetable stock or water

1 can (19 oz/540 mL) chickpeas, drained and rinsed

3 tomatoes, chopped (or one 19 oz/ 540 mL can diced or whole tomatoes with their juice)

1 large sweet potato, peeled and diced

1 large carrot, peeled and diced

¼ to ⅓ cup (60 to 80 mL) crunchy or smooth peanut butter

¼ cup (60 mL) finely chopped cilantro stems (reserve the leaves for garnish)

1 handful torn or chopped kale or Swiss chard leaves, center ribs and stems removed, or spinach (optional)

Plain yogurt, chopped peanuts and/or cilantro leaves for garnish

1. To make the soup on the stovetop, heat the oil in a large pot over medium heat. Add the onion. Cook, stirring often, until the onion has softened.

2. Add the ginger, garlic and jalapeños. Cook, stirring, for 1 to 2 minutes.

3. Add the chili powder, cumin and salt. Cook, stirring, for 1 minute.

4. Add the stock, chickpeas, tomatoes, sweet potato, carrot, peanut butter and cilantro stems. Bring to a boil.

5. Reduce the heat and simmer, uncovered, until the vegetables are tender, 20 to 30 minutes. Stir in the kale (if using) and cook until it wilts, 2 to 3 minutes.

6. To go the slow cooker route, toss everything, except the kale and oil, into the bowl of a slow cooker. Cover and cook on low for about 6 hours.

7. Uncover and stir, breaking up some of the chunks of sweet potato with the back of a spoon. Stir in the kale (if using), then put the lid back on until the kale wilts, 1 to 2 minutes.

8. Ladle out piping hot bowlfuls and serve topped with yogurt or peanuts or cilantro, or all of the above.

Vietnamese Beef Pho

Sandi McCrory, Soup Sister

Makes about 8 servings

2-inch (5 cm) piece fresh ginger

24 cups (6 L) water

8 lb (3.5 kg) beef chuck and knuckle bones

3 onions, peeled but left whole

3 Tbsp (45 mL) granulated sugar

3 Tbsp (45 mL) fish sauce or soy sauce

10 whole star anise

6 whole cloves

1 Tbsp (15 mL) salt

Pepper to taste

1 lb (500 g) thin rice noodles, cooked and drained

½ lb (250 g) raw beef sirloin or rare roast beef from the deli, sliced as thinly as possible

Toppings (optional)

Lime wedges

Bean sprouts

Finely chopped cilantro

Finely chopped fresh basil

Thinly sliced green onions

Thinly sliced Thai bird's eye chilies

A trip to Vietnam developed my love of pho (Vietnamese noodle soup). After trying various recipes, I have come to rely on this one. It was given to me by a Vietnamese Canadian (whose name I don't know) who was kind enough to dictate the instructions as I waited for an appointment. She emphasized that everyone in Vietnam has their own signature recipe for pho.
—Sandi McCrory

1. Char the piece of ginger on all sides by holding it with tongs over a gas flame or grilling it over a preheated barbecue.

2. In a very large pot, bring the water to a boil.

3. In a second large pot, combine the beef chuck and bones with enough cold water to cover them. Bring to a boil. Cook for 10 minutes.

4. Remove the beef chuck and bones with tongs and put in the very large pot of boiling water. Add the ginger, onions, sugar and fish sauce to the pot.

5. Reduce the heat and simmer, covered, for about 1½ hours. Use a large metal spoon to occasionally skim off any impurities that float to the surface.

6. Wrap the star anise and cloves in a cheesecloth bag and tie securely with kitchen string. Add the spices to the pot. Simmer for 30 minutes. Remove the beef chuck and bones, onions, ginger and spices. Add the salt and pepper to taste.

7. Just before serving, bring the broth to a rolling boil.

8. Meanwhile, put the toppings (if using) into individual serving bowls. Divide the hot cooked noodles among the soup bowls. Top the noodles with the sirloin. Ladle the broth into the soup bowls (the broth will cook the raw meat). Serve with the toppings so everyone can garnish the soup as they like.

Velvet Corn Soup

Verna Kelso and Sharlene Steele, Soup Sisters

Makes about 6 servings

*In the '70s, my mom,
Verna Kelso, took
a Chinese cooking
course from a chef
whose family had
been one of the first to
emigrate from China
to Vancouver. This
recipe is a variation
of one of the dishes
Mom learned to make.
Growing up, I couldn't
stomach creamed corn
but somehow I loved
this soup! I remember
its being a comfort
on a cold, rainy day
in Vancouver, when
Mom would always
add leftover ham from
the night before.
—Sharlene Steele*

3 cups (750 mL) chicken stock

2 cans (each 14 oz/398 mL) cream-style corn

1 cup (250 mL) drained canned or frozen corn kernels

1 green onion, chopped

1 tsp (5 mL) soy sauce

2 Tbsp (30 mL) cornstarch

2 Tbsp (30 mL) cold water

¼ cup (60 mL) finely chopped barbecued pork or cooked ham

2 egg whites

2 Tbsp (30 mL) milk

Pepper to taste

1. In a large pot, bring the stock to a boil over high heat.

2. Add the creamed corn, corn kernels, green onion and soy sauce.

3. Reduce the heat and simmer, covered, to blend the flavors, about 5 minutes.

4. In a small bowl, stir together the cornstarch and water until smooth.

5. Bring the soup back to a boil. Add the cornstarch mixture. Cook, stirring constantly, until the soup has thickened and becomes clear.

6. Stir in the pork.

7. In a small bowl, whisk the egg whites with a fork until frothy. Whisk in the milk.

8. Remove the pot from the heat and immediately pour in the egg-white mixture while slowly stirring in one direction.

9. Season with pepper to taste. Ladle the sunny soup into bowls.

Wedding Soup

Lidia Matticchio Bastianich, Chef, Restaurant Owner, Cookbook Author and Host of lidiasitaly.com

Makes about 6 servings

1 small onion, cut into chunks

2 small stalks celery with leaves, cut into chunks

1 small carrot, peeled and cut into chunks

¼ cup (60 mL) lightly packed fresh basil leaves

2 plump cloves garlic, peeled

3 Tbsp (45 mL) extra virgin olive oil

14 cups (3.5 L) cold water

½ head escarole (about 8 oz/250 g), cut into ½-inch (1 cm) slices

½ bunch Swiss chard (about 8 oz/250 g), cut into ½-inch (1 cm) slices

1 fennel bulb (about 8 oz/250 g), trimmed and cut into ¼-inch (6 mm) slices

1 zucchini (about 8 oz/250 g), cut into ½-inch (1 cm) pieces

1 Tbsp (15 mL) salt

Meatballs

2 oz (60 g) stale country bread, crusts removed (about 2 slices)

¼ cup (60 mL) milk, or more as needed

8 oz (250 g) sweet Italian sausage (without fennel seeds)

1 egg yolk, beaten

1 Tbsp (15 mL) finely chopped flat-leaf parsley

¼ tsp (1 mL) salt

Pepper to taste

12 cups (3 L) water

Additional finely chopped flat-leaf parsley for garnish

Freshly grated pecorino cheese, plus more for serving

Best-quality extra virgin olive oil for garnish

1. For the soup, pulse the onion, celery, carrot, basil and garlic in a food processor until a smooth paste (pestata) forms.

2. In a large pot, heat the oil over high heat. Scrape in the pestata. Cook, stirring, until the pestata has dried out and just begins to stick to the bottom of the pot, about 5 minutes.

cont'd on page 59

3. Add the water and stir well. Cover and bring to a boil.

4. Reduce the heat and simmer to blend the flavors, about 15 minutes.

5. Stir in the escarole, chard, fennel, zucchini and salt. Return to a simmer, and cook, covered, until the greens are tender, about 45 minutes.

6. Remove the lid and cook at a brisk simmer until the soup has reduced a bit in volume and the flavors are concentrated, about 45 minutes.

7. Meanwhile, for the meatballs, tear the bread into chunks. In a small bowl, combine the bread with just enough milk to cover it. Let soak until completely saturated.

8. Lift the bread out of the bowl and squeeze out and discard the milk. Tear the moistened bread into shreds and put in a medium bowl.

9. Remove the sausages from their casings. Crumble the meat into the bread, breaking up any clumps with your fingers.

10. Add the egg yolk, parsley, salt and pepper. Fold, toss and squeeze all the ingredients through your fingers to distribute them evenly.

11. Scoop up a small amount of the meat mixture—about a heaping teaspoonful (5 mL)—and roll it in your palms to form a 1-inch (2.5 cm) ball (the size of a large grape). Continue to form balls until all the meat is used up, putting meatballs on a large plate as you form them.

12. Meanwhile, pour the water into a second large pot and salt it lightly. Bring to a boil over high heat.

13. Drop in the meatballs, cover the pot and return the water quickly to a boil. Reduce the heat so the water simmers gently. Poach the meatballs, uncovered, until cooked through, about 5 minutes.

14. With a slotted spoon, remove the meatballs from the pot, let drain briefly then drop them into the finished soup.

15. Bring the soup to a simmer, and cook the meatballs and soup together for about 5 minutes.

16. Ladle the soup into warm bowls. Sprinkle each serving with parsley and some of the grated cheese, and drizzle with your best olive oil. Pass more cheese at the table.

This recipe is adapted from Lidia's Favorite Recipes *by Lidia Matticchio Bastianich and Tania Bastianich Manuali (Knopf, 2012).*

Wedding soup (minestra maritata) hails from Basilicata, a region in Southern Italy to which I dedicated a whole chapter in Lidia Cooks from the Heart of Italy. *Anyone with the slightest bit of Italian heritage has enjoyed wedding soup (though not always at a wedding). Many other cultures have similar soups. This is one of my favorites, and with some crusty bread it can become a complete meal.*
—Lidia Matticchio Bastianich

WINTER

Winter, with its icy blasts and snowy weather, is the most vital time to be supporting women, children and youth in crisis. This is when soup becomes most comforting to make and receive. The warmth it creates with every scrumptious mouthful both nurtures and nourishes.

In November, we hold our annual fundraising and awareness event, The Big Stir, which produces 1,200 servings of soup for Calgary's women's shelters in one night! From Mom's Minestrone to Southwestern Black Bean Soup, every bowl of homemade goodness reminds our recipients that their community cares about them.

And, because the shelters we support are multicultural, you'll find soups in this chapter from countries as far-flung as Ireland, Romania, India and Hong Kong.

Amy's Lump Soup

Carolyn Sainchuk, Soup Sister

Makes about 6 servings

Dumplings

1½ cups (375 mL) all-purpose flour

2 tsp (10 mL) baking powder

½ tsp (2 mL) salt

⅔ cup (160 mL) milk, water reserved
  from boiling potatoes, or water

2 Tbsp (30 mL) vegetable oil

1 egg, lightly beaten

Soup

2 Tbsp (30 mL) vegetable oil

2 cups (500 mL) peeled and diced
  carrots

1 cup (250 mL) finely chopped onion

1 cup (250 mL) diced celery

12 cups (3 L) chicken stock (approx.)

½ cup (125 mL) finely chopped fresh
  parsley

¼ cup (60 mL) finely chopped fresh
  dill

Salt and pepper to taste

3 cups (750 mL) cooked, diced chicken

Chopped green onions for garnish

This soup was probably originally called dumpling soup, but my family coined the name Lump Soup and it stuck. My mom's secret was to make the stock from a stewing hen. There's nothing like the low, slow percolating of an old hen to make today's chickens seem a little one-dimensional. My mom's method for making the lumps was a little sketchy, so I used my Auntie Stevie's more detailed recipe. I should probably have spent more time watching than eating!
—Carolyn Sainchuk

1. For the dumplings, whisk together the flour, baking powder and salt in a medium bowl. Make a well in the center of the dry ingredients.

2. Add the milk, oil and egg to the well. Mix to form a moist, stiff batter, like a pasta dough. Set aside.

3. For the soup, heat the oil in a large pot over medium heat. Add the carrots, onion and celery. Cook, stirring often, until the onion has softened.

4. Add 12 cups (3 L) stock, parsley, dill, and salt and pepper to taste. Bring to a rolling boil (this is important).

5. Stick a metal teaspoon into the boiling broth to heat it.

6. Using the hot spoon, scoop teaspoonfuls of the batter into the boiling soup. The dumplings need to be small because they will expand.

7. When the dumplings have all risen to the surface of the soup, add the chicken and green onions. (You can add more stock to extend this soup to feed a larger crowd.)

8. Ladle out yummy bowlfuls, making sure everyone gets an equal number of "lumps."

Brenda's Chili

Brenda Searle, Soup Sister

Makes about 6 servings

3 Tbsp (45 mL) olive oil
2 onions, finely chopped
2 carrots, peeled and diced
2 stalks celery, diced
2 sweet red peppers, seeded and diced
2 cloves garlic, minced
1 tsp (5 mL) chili powder
1 tsp (5 mL) ground cinnamon
1 tsp (5 mL) ground cumin
1 lb (500 g) extra-lean ground beef
1 can (28 oz/796 mL) diced tomatoes with
   their juice

1 can (19 oz/540 mL) chickpeas, drained
   and rinsed
1 can (19 oz/540 mL) red kidney beans,
   drained and rinsed
1 can (14 oz/398 mL) crushed tomatoes
Water as required
2 Tbsp (30 mL) balsamic vinegar
Salt and pepper to taste
½ cup (125 mL) sour cream for garnish
Grated cheese for garnish
Parsley for garnish

My children grew up on this awesome, hearty meal in a bowl. It's easy and delicious, but the best part of the story is, when my kids left for university, they asked for the recipe and made it for themselves and their friends!
—Brenda Searle

This recipe is not quite a soup, but huge pots of it are made at our events right across the country. It's a Soup Sisters and Broth Brothers favorite that's delivered to shelters at least 15 times each month.
—Sharon Hapton

1. In a large pot, heat the oil over medium heat. Add the onions, carrots, celery, peppers and garlic. Cook, stirring often, until the onions are golden brown.

2. Stir in the chili powder, cinnamon and cumin.

3. Add the beef. Cook, stirring to break the beef up into small pieces, until it is no longer pink.

4. Add the diced tomatoes, chickpeas, kidney beans and crushed tomatoes. Add water, if necessary, to make sure all the ingredients are submerged.

5. Bring to a boil over high heat. Reduce the heat and simmer, covered and stirring occasionally, until thickened, about 1 hour.

6. Stir in the vinegar and season with salt and pepper to taste.

7. Ladle up a thick and chunky bowl and garnish with a sloppy dollop of sour cream, some grated cheese and parsley.

Chili sans Carne

Zoe Polsky, Soup Sister

Makes about 6 servings

2 pkgs (each 12 oz/340 g) meatless ground round, such as Yves Veggie Cuisine
1 can (28 oz/796 mL) diced tomatoes with their juice
1 cup (250 mL) chili sauce
1 tsp (5 mL) dried oregano leaves
1 tsp (5 mL) ground cumin
1 tsp (5 mL) chili powder
1 tsp (5 mL) packed brown sugar
Salt and pepper to taste
1 can (19 oz/540 mL) red kidney beans, drained and rinsed
1 can (19 oz/540 mL) black beans, drained and rinsed
1 can (19 oz/540 mL) chickpeas, drained and rinsed
2 carrots, peeled and diced
2 stalks celery, diced
1 large onion, finely chopped
4 cloves garlic, minced

I like to serve this hearty vegetarian dish with a warm baguette and a crisp salad.
—Zoe Polsky

1. In a large pot over medium heat, cook the ground round, stirring often, until browned.

2. Stir in the tomatoes, chili sauce, oregano, cumin, chili powder, brown sugar, and salt and pepper to taste.

3. Add the kidney beans, black beans, chickpeas, carrots, celery, onion and garlic. Bring to a boil.

4. Reduce the heat and simmer, covered, until the vegetables are tender, about 1 hour.

5. Ladle up hearty, healthy bowlfuls.

Chorizo, White Bean and Kale Soup

Daniel Wagner, Owner, Rain City Soups, Vancouver

Makes about 8 servings

1 Tbsp (15 mL) olive oil

4 dry-cured chorizo sausages (each
6 inches/15 cm), diced

2 onions, finely chopped

2 carrots, peeled and diced

2 stalks celery, diced

1 cup (250 mL) peeled, seeded and diced
squash (such as butternut or acorn)

3 cloves garlic, minced

Pinch of salt

2 Tbsp (30 mL) Spanish sweet smoked
paprika

8 cups (2 L) water

1 can (28 oz/796 mL) San Marzano
tomatoes, puréed, with their juice, in a
blender (see sidebar)

1 can (19 oz/540 mL) white beans,
drained and rinsed

1 can (5½ oz/156 mL) tomato paste

Pepper to taste

4 cups (1 L) thinly sliced kale, center ribs
and stems removed (1 large bunch)

Pesto (optional)

San Marzano tomatoes are a variety of plum tomatoes thought by many to make the very best sauce. They have a stronger flavor and are less acidic than regular plum tomatoes. Look for canned San Marzanos in Italian grocery stores or specialty food stores.

1. In a large pot, heat the oil over medium-high heat. Add the chorizo. Cook, stirring often, until the chorizo is beginning to brown.

2. Add the onions, carrots, celery, squash, garlic and a pinch of salt. Cook, stirring often, until the onion starts to soften.

3. Add the paprika. Cook, stirring, to develop the flavors, 1 to 2 minutes.

4. Add the water, tomatoes, beans, tomato paste, and salt and pepper to taste. Bring to a boil.

5. Reduce the heat and simmer, covered, for 1 hour.

6. Add the kale. Simmer, uncovered, for 30 minutes.

7. Season with salt and pepper to taste. Ladle up hearty bowlfuls, add a swirl of pesto (if using) to each, and enjoy.

This is the soup that inspired me to start my own soup company. It's a variation of a classic Portuguese soup called caldo verde *that my wonderful nanny used to prepare. Over the years I served this to all my friends and they kept telling me I had to start selling it. It's still my all-time favorite soup to make and eat. I love it with garlic bread.*
—Daniel Wagner

Everyday Lentil Soup

Vikram Vij, Chef/Co-Owner, Vij's and Rangoli, Vancouver

Makes about 4 servings

Look for chana
dal, urad dal,
black mustard and
fenugreek seeds and
curry leaves (see
page 121) in your local
Indian grocery store.

¼ cup (60 mL) tamarind pulp

⅓ cup (80 mL) warm water

¼ cup (60 mL) yellow lentils (chana dal), picked over and rinsed

2 Tbsp (30 mL) vegetable oil, divided

1 tsp (5 mL) split black lentils (urad dal), picked over, rinsed and divided

¼ fresh coconut, shelled and finely grated

3 long dried red chilies, broken into pieces

1½ Tbsp (22 mL) coriander seeds

5 sprigs fresh curry leaves (see page 121), leaves picked off and divided

4¼ cups (1.06 L) cold water (approx.), divided

½ tsp (2 mL) black mustard seeds

25 small red shallots, peeled but left whole

2 small fresh green chilies, halved lengthwise

½ tsp (2 mL) salt

1½ tsp (7 mL) finely grated palm sugar or brown sugar

½ tsp (2 mL) fenugreek seeds, toasted

2 cups (500 mL) cubed mixed vegetables (see note)

1. In a small bowl, soak the tamarind pulp in the warm water for 10 minutes. Strain through a fine-mesh sieve into another bowl, discarding the fibers in the sieve. Set aside.

2. In a medium saucepan, combine the yellow lentils with enough water to cover them generously. Bring to a boil.

3. Reduce the heat and simmer, uncovered, until the lentils are tender, about 15 minutes. Drain well, mash until smooth and set aside.

4. Meanwhile, in a small heavy-bottomed saucepan, heat 1 Tbsp (15 mL) oil over medium heat. Add ½ tsp (2 mL) black lentils. Cook, stirring often, until the lentils begin to brown, about 4 minutes.

5. Add the coconut, dried red chilies, coriander seeds and three-quarters of the curry leaves. Cook, stirring often, until the coconut is golden brown, about 4 minutes.

6. Remove the saucepan from the heat and let cool slightly. Tip the lentil mixture into a mortar and add ¼ cup (60 mL) cold water. Grind with a pestle until a paste forms. (This mixture is called a masala.)

7. In a large pot, heat the remaining oil over medium heat. Add the mustard seeds. Cook just until the seeds begin to pop, 2 to 3 minutes.

8. Add the remaining black lentils. Cook, stirring, for 1 minute.

9. Add the shallots, green chilies, salt and the remaining curry leaves. Cook, stirring often, until aromatic, about 5 minutes.

10. Add the strained tamarind liquid, palm sugar and fenugreek seeds. Cook, stirring often, until the raw aroma of the tamarind disappears, about 5 minutes.

11. Stir in the mashed yellow lentils and the masala. Cook, stirring often, for the flavors to blend, about 5 minutes, adding a little more water, if necessary, if the mixture is too dry.

12. Add the mixed vegetables and the remaining cold water. Bring to a boil.

13. Reduce the heat and simmer, covered, until the vegetables are just tender, about 15 minutes. Season with more salt to taste (the soup should be on the salty side).

14. Ladle into bowls and enjoy.

This thick lentil soup is healthy and a little spicy. For best flavor, use a combination of eggplant, carrots, green beans, pumpkin and sweet potato.
—Vikram Vij

Green Soup

Rosie Daykin, Owner, Butter Baked Goods, Vancouver, and
Cookbook Author

Makes about 6 servings

3 Tbsp (45 mL) olive oil
2 leeks (white parts only), finely chopped
2 Tbsp (30 mL) peeled and finely minced fresh ginger
1 bunch kale (about 12 stalks), center ribs and stems removed,
    leaves coarsely chopped
3 cups (750 mL) lightly packed baby spinach
6 cups (1.5 L) vegetable stock
2 Tbsp (30 mL) miso paste
2 Tbsp (30 mL) almond butter
Finely grated zest of 1 lemon
Salt and pepper to taste
Plain yogurt for garnish
¼ cup (60 mL) finely chopped fresh mint for garnish

1. In a large, heavy-bottomed pot, heat the oil over medium heat. Add the leeks and ginger. Cook, stirring often, until the leeks have softened.

2. Add the kale and spinach and cook, stirring occasionally, until the kale is very tender, 12 to 15 minutes.

3. Add the stock, miso paste and almond butter, and bring to a boil.

4. Reduce the heat and simmer, covered, for about 15 minutes.

5. Stir in the lemon zest and season generously with salt and pepper to taste.

6. Purée the soup until smooth, if you like, or leave as is. Reheat gently.

7. Ladle into bowls and top with a nice dollop of plain yogurt and a sprinkling of chopped fresh mint.

One summer my daughter India and I became addicted to green juice, a wonderful concoction of kale, apple, mint and ginger. I got to thinking that, as easy as it is to begin a sunny day with a refreshing glass of kale, come rainy November, it might not seem so appealing, and I came up with this soup to enjoy during the winter.
—Rosie Daykin

Green Split Pea Soup

Gordie Fehr, Broth Brother

Makes about 8 servings

4 cups (1 L) chicken stock

2 cups (500 mL) green split peas, picked over and rinsed

1 ham bone

2 cans (each 10 oz/284 mL) condensed chicken broth

1 cup (250 mL) diced smoked ham

2/3 cup (160 mL) finely chopped onion

1/2 cup (125 mL) sliced celery

1/4 cup (60 mL) peeled and sliced carrot

1 clove garlic, minced

2 parsley sprigs

1 bay leaf

1/2 tsp (2 mL) granulated sugar

1/4 tsp (1 mL) salt

1/8 tsp (0.5 mL) dried thyme leaves

1/8 tsp (0.5 mL) pepper

Chopped parsley for garnish

1. In a large pot, combine the chicken stock, split peas and ham bone. Bring to a boil.

2. Reduce the heat and simmer, covered, for 45 minutes.

3. Add the chicken broth, smoked ham, onion, celery, carrot, garlic, parsley, bay leaf, sugar, salt, thyme and pepper. Bring to a boil.

4. Reduce the heat and simmer, covered, for 1 1/2 hours.

5. Remove the parsley stems and bay leaf. Add a little water if the soup is too thick.

6. Ladle into soup bowls and garnish with parsley. Serve, savor and lick your lips!

This recipe was created by my wife Marilyn's grandmother, Maude Fitzpatrick. We estimate it dates back to the late 1940s. I have tinkered with it a little by using chicken stock instead of water.
—Gordie Fehr

Our honorary Broth Brother, Gordie Fehr, celebrated his 80th birthday in Ottawa with his children and grandchildren by providing hundreds of liters of delicious soup in support of the women and children at Oshki Kizis Lodge. He has been an avid soup maker all his life.
—Sharon Hapton

Hot and Sour Chicken Soup with Leeks

Lesley Stowe, Chef/Owner, Lesley Stowe Fine Foods, Vancouver

Makes about 6 servings

8 cups (2 L) chicken stock
2 large boneless, skinless chicken breasts
1 cup (250 mL) thinly sliced leeks (white parts only)
2 Tbsp (30 mL) minced fresh ginger
5 Tbsp (75 mL) Chinese black vinegar (see sidebar) or Worcestershire sauce
1 Tbsp (15 mL) apple cider vinegar
½ tsp (2 mL) pepper
2 small baby bok choy, sliced
3 to 4 fresh radishes, thinly sliced
2 tsp (10 mL) sesame oil
¼ cup (60 mL) cilantro leaves
Thinly sliced red chilies to taste (see sidebar; optional)

1. In a medium pot, combine the stock and chicken breasts. Bring to a boil.

2. Reduce the heat and simmer, uncovered, for 10 minutes.

3. Remove the pot from the heat. Let stand, covered, for 10 minutes.

4. Remove the breasts from the pot, reserving the stock. When cool enough to handle, shred the chicken breasts, keeping the pieces a fairly good size. Set aside.

5. Strain the stock through a fine-mesh sieve into a clean pot. Add the leeks, ginger, black vinegar, cider vinegar and pepper. Bring to a boil.

6. Reduce the heat and simmer, uncovered, until the leeks are tender, about 15 minutes.

7. Add the bok choy and radishes. Simmer for 5 minutes.

8. Add the shredded chicken and sesame oil.

9. Ladle up steaming bowlfuls and scatter each portion with cilantro leaves and chilies (if using) to taste.

If your town has an Asian market, it's worth venturing out for the black vinegar, an inexpensive yet delicious addition to traditional Chinese dishes. Note: the red chilies pack quite a punch, so adjust the amount to your liking or serve on the side for guests who may not like their soup quite this hot!

This soup is exactly what I crave when the dull days of January descend upon the "Wet" Coast. It's comforting and light with a good kick of spice from the chilies, and warms you up from the inside out. Feel free to improvise with your favorite vegetables—carrots cut in julienne strips or cremini mushrooms (baby portobellos) make excellent additions.
—Lesley Stowe

Irish Coddle

Sheila Alwell, Soup Sister

Makes about 6 servings

2 Tbsp (30 mL) vegetable oil

12 oz (375 g) sliced peameal bacon

1 lb (500 g) pork sausages

6 medium potatoes, peeled and cut into large chunks

2 carrots, peeled and chopped

1 large onion, halved and thinly sliced

2 cloves garlic, minced

Salt and pepper to taste

4 cups (1 L) chicken stock

1 tsp (5 mL) dried thyme leaves

1 bay leaf

1 Tbsp (15 mL) finely chopped parsley

1. In a large pot over medium-high heat, heat the oil and cook the bacon until the edges are just beginning to turn brown. Transfer to paper towels to drain.

2. Add the sausages to the pot. Cook, turning often, until the sausages are browned (the sausages won't be completely cooked). Transfer to paper towels to drain.

3. Add the potatoes, carrots, onion, garlic, and salt and pepper to taste to the pot. Cook, stirring often, until the onion starts to soften.

4. Add the stock, thyme and bay leaf. Bring to a boil.

5. Reduce the heat and simmer, covered, for 15 minutes.

6. Meanwhile, cut the bacon and sausages into chunks.

7. Add the bacon and sausages to the pot. Simmer, covered, until the sausages are cooked and the potatoes are tender, about 30 minutes. Remove the bay leaf. Stir in the parsley.

8. Ladle up piping hot bowlfuls and serve with warm crusty dinner rolls.

This comfort food is inexpensive, easy to prepare and quick to cook. In the days when Catholics were not supposed to eat meat on Fridays, this meal was often eaten on Thursdays, allowing a family to use up any remaining sausages or bacon. My generation grew up on this stew, a very welcoming dish during the cold days of winter.
—Sheila Alwell

Lentil Soup with Porcini Mushrooms and Red Wine

Karen Barnaby, Product Development Chef, Gordon Food Service, Delta, B.C.

Makes about 8 servings

1½ cups (375 mL) red wine

½ cup (125 mL) dried porcini mushrooms

1¼ lb (625 g) Puy lentils (see sidebar), picked over and rinsed

¼ cup (60 mL) olive oil

3 cups (750 mL) finely chopped onions

1½ cups (375 mL) peeled and diced carrots

1½ cups (375 mL) diced celery

8 cloves garlic, coarsely chopped

2 Tbsp (30 mL) finely chopped fresh rosemary

2 Tbsp (30 mL) finely chopped fresh sage

Salt to taste

1½ tsp (7 mL) ground coriander

⅛ tsp (0.5 mL) ground allspice

⅓ cup (80 mL) tomato paste

8 to 12 cups (2 to 3 L) water

Pepper to taste

Extra virgin olive oil for garnish

Puy lentils are small, grayish green lentils from France. Look for them in larger grocery stores or specialty food stores.

1. One hour before you start to make the soup, combine the wine and mushrooms in a nonreactive bowl. In another bowl, combine the lentils with enough water to cover them by 1 inch (2.5 cm).

2. In a large pot, heat the oil over medium heat. Add the onions, carrots, celery, garlic, rosemary, sage and salt to taste. Cook, stirring often, until the onions have softened.

3. Add the coriander and allspice and cook, stirring, for 1 minute. Stir in the tomato paste.

4. Drain the lentils and add them to the pot, along with 8 cups (1 L) of water. Bring to a boil.

5. Meanwhile, remove the mushrooms from the wine and chop them coarsely. Add the mushrooms to the soup along with the wine, pouring carefully to avoid adding the sediment at the bottom of the bowl.

6. Reduce the heat and simmer until the lentils are very tender, about 1 hour, adding more water if necessary to keep it simmering.

7. Purée the soup until smooth. Reheat gently. Is it too thick? Add more water. Too thin? Let it simmer until it thickens. When it's the right consistency, season with salt and pepper to taste.

8. Serve bowlfuls of the earthy soup with a generous squiggle of extra virgin olive oil on top.

The combination of earthy lentils, porcini mushrooms and tangy red wine is a study in balance. Get it right, like it is here, and you'll be richly rewarded with a wonderful bowl of soup.
—Karen Barnaby

Lynda's Chicken Soup

Lynda T. Rathburn, Soup Sister

Makes about 6 servings

¼ cup (60 mL) olive oil
1 cup (250 mL) diced celery
¾ cup (185 mL) finely chopped onion
½ cup (125 mL) peeled and diced carrot
1 cup (250 mL) peeled and diced potato
5 cups (1.25 L) chicken stock
2 jalapeño chilies, seeded and finely chopped
½ tsp (2 mL) salt
Pepper to taste
1 can (19 oz/540 mL) lentils, drained and rinsed
1 cup (250 mL) diced cooked chicken
2 Tbsp (30 mL) finely chopped fresh oregano (see sidebar)

If fresh oregano isn't available, substitute 1 Tbsp (15 mL) dried oregano leaves, but add it along with the chicken stock.

1. In a large pot, heat the oil over medium heat. Add the celery, onion and carrot. Cook, stirring often, until the onion has softened. With a slotted spoon, remove the vegetables and set aside.

2. Add the potato to the oil remaining in the pot. Cook, stirring often, until browned and crisp.

3. Return the sautéed vegetables to the pot, along with the stock. Add the jalapeños and season with salt and pepper to taste. Bring to a boil.

4. Reduce the heat and simmer, covered, until the vegetables are tender, about 30 minutes.

5. Add the lentils and chicken. Cook until heated through, about 5 minutes.

6. Stir in the oregano. Ladle the soup into bowls and enjoy.

My children have always liked roast chicken, so the obvious next step was making them chicken soup. When they were young, I kept said soup fairly simple. But after a while, simple can become boring, so it was time to jazz it up! This soup was the result and became reason enough to roast a chicken.
—Lynda T. Rathburn

Lynda's Chicken Soup with Cream and Corn

Add an 11-ounce (311 mL) drained can of corn niblets and 1 cup (250 mL) of half-and-half cream (10% MF) to the soup when you add the chicken, then sprinkle each serving with shredded Monterey Jack cheese and serve the soup with cornbread.

Mom's Minestrone

Michele Chandler, Soup Sister and Purveyor at The Art of Pudding

Makes about 6 servings

2 Tbsp (30 mL) olive oil
1 Spanish onion, coarsely chopped
3 cloves garlic, minced
3 large carrots, peeled and diced
2 stalks celery, diced
10 cups (2.5 L) chicken stock
¼ head of savoy or green cabbage, shredded
2 cups (500 mL) trimmed and chopped green beans
1 potato, unpeeled and diced
1 zucchini, diced
¾ cup (185 mL) dried baby lima beans (see sidebar), picked over and rinsed
⅓ cup (80 mL) tomato paste
2 to 3 Parmesan cheese rinds (see sidebar)
Salt and pepper to taste

1. In a large pot, heat the oil over medium-high heat. Add the onion and garlic. Cook, stirring often, until the onion is golden brown.

2. Add the carrots and celery. Cook, stirring often, for 5 minutes.

3. Add the stock, cabbage, green beans, potato, zucchini, lima beans and tomato paste. Bring to a boil.

4. Reduce the heat and simmer, partially covered, for 2 hours.

5. Add the Parmesan rinds. Simmer, partially covered, for 1 hour.

6. Season with salt and pepper to taste. Ladle up hearty veggie-full bowls.

Keep your Parmesan rinds frozen until needed for the soup, or ask your cheese store for a couple.

I come from a long line of foodies. My mother, Elizabeth Brogli, was the daughter of Caesar Brogli, head maître d' at the Ritz Hotel in London, U.K. This was her favorite Italian soup and a weekly staple on the stove in the winter months. The secret is using dried baby lima beans. Unlike other dried pulses, they don't need presoaking and they're just the right size for a spoonful of soup.
—Michele Chandler

Mulligatawny

Karl Jarrett, Chef and Broth Brother

Makes about 8 servings

Mulligatawny is an Anglo-Indian soup based on a traditional Tamil stew. It was created by the Tamil servants of the British Raj, who demanded a soup course from a cuisine that had never produced one. The name mulligatawny comes from a Tamil word meaning "pepper water."

Although this isn't a traditional mulligatawny, I spent some time perfecting my own, modernized version. The result is a rich soup with a punchy, house-filling aroma and a powerful explosion of soul-warming flavor.
—Karl Jarrett

3 Tbsp (45 mL) olive oil
3 Tbsp (45 mL) ghee (see page 46) or butter
2 onions, finely chopped
2 stalks celery, diced
1 carrot, peeled and diced
3 cloves garlic, minced
1 Tbsp (15 mL) mild, medium or hot curry powder
1 tsp (5 mL) fresh thyme leaves
½ tsp (2 mL) red chili flakes
½ tsp (2 mL) ground cinnamon
½ tsp (2 mL) ground coriander
½ tsp (2 mL) ground cumin
Seeds of 3 whole cardamom pods, crushed

2 skinless, boneless chicken breasts, cut into bite-size pieces
1 Tbsp (15 mL) fresh lemon juice
4 cups (1 L) chicken stock
2 white potatoes, peeled and cut into ½-inch (1 cm) cubes
1 Fuji apple, peeled, cored and cut into ½-inch (1 cm) cubes
2 cans (each 14 oz/398 mL) unsweetened coconut milk (not light)
¼ cup (60 mL) basmati rice
2 Tbsp (30 mL) apple cider
1 tsp (5 mL) apple cider vinegar
¼ cup (60 mL) well-packed finely chopped cilantro
Salt and pepper to taste

1. In a large pot, heat the oil and ghee over medium-low heat. Add the onions, celery, carrot and garlic. Cook, stirring often, until the onions have softened.

2. Add the curry powder, thyme, chili flakes, cinnamon, coriander, cumin and cardamom seeds. Cook, stirring, until the spices are fragrant, about 1 minute.

3. Add the chicken. Cook, stirring often, until the outside of the chicken is no longer pink.

4. Add the lemon juice. Cook, stirring, until the lemon juice evaporates.

5. Add the stock, potatoes and apple. Bring to a boil.

6. Reduce the heat and simmer, covered, until the vegetables are tender and the chicken is no longer pink inside, about 15 minutes.

7. Add the coconut milk, rice and apple cider. Simmer, uncovered and stirring often in case the soup scorches, until the rice is tender, about 10 minutes.

8. Add the vinegar. Simmer, uncovered, until the soup is the consistency of liquid honey. Stir in the cilantro and salt and pepper to taste. Ladle up exotic bowlfuls.

Nanny's Bean Soup

Ruth Craig, Soup Sister

Makes about 6 servings

  2 cups (500 mL) dried white beans (see page 4)
  8 cups (2 L) cold water
  1 ham bone (preferably roasted), with extra meat still attached
  2 onions, cut in half
  2 carrots, unpeeled and coarsely chopped
  2 stalks celery, coarsely chopped
  1 to 2 cups (250 to 500 mL) cubed ham (from the ham bone or the deli)
  1 to 2 Tbsp (15 to 30 mL) bacon fat or olive or canola oil
  2 to 5 cloves garlic, minced (according to taste)
  2 Tbsp (30 mL) all-purpose flour
  White vinegar to taste

When we were kids, bean soup warmed us on frigid winter days like no other soup could. The white vinegar added a touch of sour to awaken the taste buds just a little more. Heaven!
—Ruth Craig

1. Soak the beans in the water (see page 4). After soaking, drain the beans, reserving the soaking water.

2. In a large pot, combine the reserved soaking water, soaked beans, ham bone, onions, carrots and celery. Bring slowly to a simmer (do not boil).

3. Reduce the heat and simmer, covered, until the beans are tender, 2 to 3 hours.

4. Remove the bone. Add the ham to the soup.

5. Meanwhile, heat the bacon fat in a large skillet over medium heat. Add the garlic. Cook, stirring, until the garlic is golden and fragrant.

6. Add the flour to the skillet and cook, stirring constantly, until smooth, bubbly and thickened.

7. Bring the soup to a boil. Add a ladleful of the liquid from the soup to the flour mixture, stirring quickly to blend. Cook, stirring, for 1 minute.

8. Repeat this step three more times.

9. Add the flour mixture to the boiling soup, stirring constantly.

10. Reduce the heat and simmer, stirring often, until the soup thickens but isn't gluey. Add a little water if the soup is too thick.

11. Ladle up hearty bowlfuls and add a little white vinegar to taste to each bowl. Serve with crusty bread.

Navy Bean, Spinach and Dill Soup

Mary Luz Mejia, Food and Travel Writer/Editor, and Culinary Curator

Makes about 4 servings

This hearty, warming soup is perfect when you want something nutritious and easy to prepare, especially when the weather is chilly and you crave comfort in a cup or bowl. It's also vegetarian and gluten free but you can, if you like, add protein to make it particularly rib-sticking—cubed cooked chicken works well.

—Mary Luz Mejia

3 Tbsp (45 mL) olive oil
1 Tbsp (15 mL) butter
2 carrots, peeled and diced
2 stalks celery, diced
2 small shallots, finely chopped
1 bay leaf
Pinch of sweet Hungarian paprika
Salt and pepper to taste
2 cups (500 mL) vegetable stock
2 cups (500 mL) water

1 can (19 oz/540 mL) navy beans, drained
   and rinsed
1 Yukon Gold potato, peeled and diced
2 cups (500 mL) lightly packed spinach,
   leaves shredded and tough stems
   removed
2 Tbsp (30 mL) finely chopped fresh dill
Baguette slices to serve
Shredded Dubliner cheese or aged
   cheddar cheese to taste

1. In a large pot, heat the oil and butter over medium-high heat. Add the carrots, celery and shallots. Cook, stirring often, until the shallots have softened.

2. Stir in the bay leaf, paprika, and salt and pepper to taste.

3. Add the stock and water. Bring to a boil.

4. Add the beans and potato.

5. Reduce the heat and simmer, covered, until the potato is tender, 10 to 15 minutes.

6. Stir in the spinach. Cook just until it wilts, 1 to 2 minutes. Stir in the dill and season with salt and pepper to taste. Remove the bay leaf.

7. Just before serving, preheat the broiler and toast the baguette slices on one side under the broiler until golden. Turn and top with cheese. Broil until the cheese has melted.

8. Ladle the soup into bowls and serve with the cheesy baguette slices.

NOtaBLE's Chicken Soup

Michael Noble, Chef/Owner, NOtaBLE the Restaurant, Calgary

Makes about 4 servings

2 Tbsp (30 mL) olive oil
2 Tbsp (30 mL) cold butter, cut into cubes
½ onion, finely chopped
2 cloves garlic, minced
1 carrot, peeled and diced
½ leek (white part only), thinly sliced
¼ sweet red pepper, seeded and diced
2 sprigs thyme
Pinch of red chili flakes
Salt and pepper to taste
6 cups (1.5 L) hot chicken or vegetable stock
1 small bay leaf

1. In a large pot over medium heat, heat the oil and butter until foamy.

2. Add the onion and garlic. Cook, stirring often, until the onion has softened but is not brown.

3. Add the carrot, leek, red pepper, thyme, chili flakes, and salt and pepper to taste. Cook, stirring often, until the vegetables start to soften.

4. Add the hot chicken stock and bay leaf. Bring to a boil.

5. Reduce the heat and simmer, uncovered, until the vegetables are tender, about 20 minutes.

6. Remove the thyme stems and bay leaf. Season with salt and pepper to taste. Ladle out steaming bowlfuls and dig in.

Add diced leftover roast chicken, small cooked pasta or green peas to this soup, if you like, and garnish with chopped chives or flat-leaf parsley, or both. Serve with a hearty grilled cheese sandwich for an easy, satisfying lunch.
—Michael Noble

Phamie's Famous Scotch Broth

Fiona Buchanan, Soup Sister

Makes about 4 servings

My grandmother Euphamia (known as Phamie) Ogilvie Hughes Dickson made a perfect cup of tea and the best homemade soup. I was one of eight grandchildren who regularly visited her. At the end of each visit, she would squeeze a £5 note into my hand, give me a big hug and whisper, "I love you the most but you mustn't tell the others." Only after she died did we learn she conducted this little ritual with all eight of us.
—Fiona Buchanan

5 cups (1.25 L) water
1 beef bone for soup
1½ Tbsp (22 mL) pearl barley, rinsed and drained
1 tsp (5 mL) dried thyme leaves
1 tsp (5 mL) dried oregano leaves
Salt and pepper to taste
2 cups (500 mL) peeled and diced carrots
2 cups (500 mL) peeled and diced rutabaga
2 cups (500 mL) peeled and diced potatoes
½ cup (125 mL) chopped leek (white part only)
1 cup (250 mL) shredded cabbage
1 cup (250 mL) frozen peas
2 Tbsp (30 mL) finely chopped parsley
Fresh parsley for garnish

1. In a large pot, combine the water, beef bone, barley, thyme, oregano, and salt and pepper to taste. Bring to a boil, using a large metal spoon to skim off any impurities that float to the surface.

2. Add the carrots, rutabaga, potatoes and leek.

3. Reduce the heat and simmer, covered, for 1 hour.

4. Add the cabbage and peas. Simmer, uncovered, until the vegetables are tender, about 10 minutes.

5. Stir in the parsley. Simmer, uncovered, for 5 minutes. Season with salt and pepper to taste.

6. Ladle up hearty bowlfuls, garnish with parsley and get a glow on. Homemade bread with lashings of butter is a nice complement to Phamie's Scotch Broth and helps polish off every last drop. Optional but recommended: a wee dram of whiskey to complete your glow!

Potato-Leek Soup

The Soup Sisters' Sisters, Founder Sharon Hapton and her sisters,
Lili Scharf and Rina Grunwald

Makes about 6 servings

¼ cup (60 mL) butter
3 large leeks (white parts only), thinly sliced
¼ cup (60 mL) all-purpose flour
7 cups (1.75 L) water
7 medium Yukon Gold potatoes, peeled, halved and thinly sliced
Salt and pepper to taste
1 cup (250 mL) whipping or table cream (35% or 18% MF)
Finely chopped parsley for garnish (optional)

1. In a large pot, melt the butter over low heat. Add the leeks. Cook, covered, until the leeks have softened, about 5 minutes.

2. Stir in the flour. Cook, stirring, for 1 minute.

3. Gradually add the water, stirring constantly to avoid lumps.

4. Add the potatoes and salt and pepper to taste. Bring to a boil, stirring constantly.

5. Reduce the heat and simmer, covered, until the potatoes are tender, about 35 minutes.

6. Add the cream. Simmer until heated through.

7. Ladle up steaming bowlfuls and scatter with parsley (if using). Bon appétit!

This soup is one of my sisters and I all remember as a favorite when we were growing up. The simple ingredients combine to create great flavor. Our mother says she used cream from an elderly aunt who got it from nearby Hutterite farmers, so heavy it had to be spooned out of the jar! The soup makes a great base for all sorts of add-ins: frozen peas and corn, shrimp or firm fish are all good.
—Sharon Hapton

Quick Bangers 'n' Beans Soup

Tanya Steel, Special Projects, epicurious.com, and Cookbook Author

Makes about 6 servings

2 Tbsp (30 mL) olive oil

1 onion, finely chopped

8 oz (250 g) cooked chicken andouille or other cooked sausages (about 2 large), thinly sliced or diced

1 medium baking or white potato (about 5 oz/150 g), peeled and diced

2 cans (each 19 oz/540 mL) cannellini beans, drained and rinsed

2 cups (500 mL) chicken stock

1½ cups (375 mL) water

1 cup (250 mL) pasta sauce

2 tsp (10 mL) finely chopped fresh rosemary (or 1 tsp/5 mL dried rosemary, crumbled)

Pepper to taste

If you're not a fan of spicy andouille sausage, you can use any type of cooked sausage in this soup, or substitute chopped smoked ham, prosciutto or cooked bacon. Freshly grated Parmesan cheese or a dab of plain yogurt mixed with a bit of chopped flat-leaf parsley both make tasty garnishes.

1. In a large pot, heat the oil over medium heat. Add the onion. Cook, stirring often, until the onion has softened but is not brown.

2. Add the sausages and potato and increase the heat to medium-high. Cook, stirring often, until the sausages are lightly browned.

3. Stir in the beans, stock, water, pasta sauce and rosemary. Bring to a boil.

4. Reduce the heat and simmer, covered, until the soup has thickened slightly, about 15 minutes.

5. Purée 1½ cups (375 mL) of the soup until smooth. Stir the puréed soup back into the pot.

6. Season with pepper to taste. Ladle up hearty bowlfuls.

Rich Oxtail and Orzo Soup with Madeira

Julia Aitken, Food Writer and Editor

Makes about 6 servings

1 large onion, coarsely chopped

1 large carrot, peeled and coarsely chopped

1 large parsnip, peeled and coarsely chopped

2 stalks celery, coarsely chopped

6 cloves garlic, unpeeled

1 Tbsp (15 mL) vegetable oil

3 lb (1.5 kg) oxtail, cut into 2-inch (5 cm) lengths

3 Tbsp (45 mL) tomato paste

1½ cups (375 mL) Madeira, divided

4 cups (1 L) beef stock

4 cups (1 L) water

1 tsp (5 mL) whole black peppercorns

3 whole star anise

3 bushy sprigs fresh thyme

3 bay leaves

½ cup (125 mL) orzo or other tiny pasta

½ cup (125 mL) whipping cream (35% MF)

2 Tbsp (30 mL) good-quality grainy mustard

Salt and pepper to taste

Tiny sprigs fresh thyme for garnish

Good butchers should have oxtail. A large tail weighs about 3 lb (1.5 kg) and, if it's not already cut into pieces, ask your butcher to do this for you.

1. Preheat the oven to 450°F (230°C).

2. In a shallow roasting pan, toss the onion, carrot, parsnip, celery and garlic with the oil.

3. Spread the pieces of oxtail with tomato paste. Nestle the oxtail among the vegetables in the roasting pan. Roast, uncovered and turning once or twice, until the oxtail is well browned, 35 to 40 minutes.

4. Tip the contents of the roasting pan into a large pot. Add 1 cup (250 mL) Madeira to the roasting pan. Set the pan over medium-high heat and bring to a boil, stirring to scrape any browned bits from the bottom of the pan. Pour the contents of the roasting pan into the pot.

5. Add the stock, water, peppercorns, star anise, thyme and bay leaves to the pot. Bring to a boil.

6. Reduce the heat and simmer, covered, until the oxtail meat is very tender, about 3 hours.

cont'd on page 92

This soup takes two days to prepare and requires a bit of work but will reward you with perhaps the most flavorsome bowlful you've ever sipped. It's guaranteed to thaw you out on the most frigid of winter days. Since the orzo absorbs more stock over time, if you want to make the soup in advance, be prepared to add extra beef stock to thin it down if necessary before serving.
—Julia Aitken

7. Using tongs, remove the oxtail to a bowl. Let cool to room temperature then refrigerate, covered, overnight.

8. Strain the stock through a fine-mesh sieve into a large bowl, pressing on the vegetables to extract as much liquid as possible. Discard the vegetables and spices. Let the stock cool to room temperature then refrigerate, covered, overnight. (For tips on chilling the soup, see page 8.)

9. The next day, remove the meat from the oxtail bones, discarding all visible fat. Finely chop the meat and set aside.

10. Carefully remove and discard the fat that has solidified on the surface of the stock. Pour the stock into a large pot and bring to a boil.

11. Add the orzo to the pot. Reduce the heat and cook, stirring occasionally, until the orzo is tender, 10 to 12 minutes.

12. Meanwhile, whip the cream until stiff peaks form. Gently fold in the mustard. Set aside.

13. Add the oxtail meat and remaining Madeira to the pot and heat through without boiling. Season with salt and pepper to taste.

14. Ladle up steaming bowlfuls. Float a fluffy spoonful of mustard cream on each and garnish with thyme.

DICED TOMATOES
TOMATES EN DÉS

2.84 L (100 fl oz)

Romanian Tripe Soup

Ramona Stelescu, Soup Sister

Makes about 6 servings

2 lb (1 kg) beef tripe

28 cups (7 L) water, divided

2 Tbsp (30 mL) apple cider vinegar

1 tsp (5 mL) salt

1 bay leaf

2 lb (1 kg) beef soup bones

2 large carrots, peeled and trimmed

1 large parsnip, peeled and trimmed

1 onion, peeled

1 small head celeriac (see page 28), peeled and quartered

3 cloves garlic, peeled

1 Tbsp (15 mL) whole black peppercorns

2/3 cup (160 mL) low-fat sour cream

1 egg yolk

Pinch of salt

Pinch of pepper

Traditional Toppings

Romanian Tripe, or *Ciorba de Burta*, is traditionally served with hot chilies on the side, along with extra sour cream and vinegar. Sometimes garlic sauce is also provided (5 to 6 cloves of garlic, mashed with salt to taste, then stirred together with ¼ cup/ 60 mL of water).

1. Place the tripe in a very large, heatproof bowl. In a large pot, bring 8 cups (2 L) of the water to a boil. Add the vinegar, salt and bay leaf.

2. Pour the boiling water over the tripe to rinse it thoroughly. Drain the tripe and rinse it under cold water.

3. Put the beef bones in the same pot. Place the tripe on top of the bones. Add the remaining 20 cups (5 L) of water. Bring slowly to a boil.

4. Reduce the heat and simmer, covered. Use a large metal spoon to skim off any impurities that float to the surface every 30 minutes. Simmer until the tripe has softened, about 2 hours.

5. Add the carrots, parsnip, onion, celeriac, garlic and peppercorns to the pot. Bring to a boil. Reduce the heat and simmer, covered, until the tripe is fork-tender, about 1 hour.

6. With a large metal spoon, skim any fat from the surface of the soup.

7. Strain through a fine-mesh sieve into a clean bowl, reserving the tripe but discarding the remaining solids.

8. Slice the tripe into thin, bite-size strips. Return the broth and tripe to the pot. Reheat gently.

9. In a medium bowl, whisk together the sour cream, egg yolk, salt and pepper.

10. Gradually whisk 2 ladlefuls of broth into the sour cream mixture until well combined. Stir the sour cream mixture back into the soup. Reheat gently (do not boil).

11. Ladle up steaming bowlfuls and enjoy!

This special recipe has been passed down through my family from my grandfather, who was a chef. We didn't have much in Communist Romania, but this soup always brought us around the table, letting us escape from the hardships, if only for a while. I still make this soup, which will forever be my family's comfort. I hope it brings you and your loved ones together, to sit, to talk, to laugh and to live.
—Ramona Stelescu

Southwestern Black Bean Soup

Massimo Capra, Chef, Restaurant Owner and Cookbook Author

Makes about 8 servings

I am a soup lover, and living in a multicultural city like Toronto has allowed me to experience cuisines from around the world. Their soups may be very different, but every culture considers its own particular chicken soup one to cure all ills. This isn't a chicken soup but, with its Tex–Mex flavors, it is one of my favorites.
—Massimo Capra

2 cups (500 mL) dried black beans (see page 4)
2 Tbsp (30 mL) vegetable oil
2 cups (500 mL) finely chopped onions
1½ cups (375 mL) seeded and diced sweet red peppers
1 cup (250 mL) peeled and finely chopped carrots
1 cup (250 mL) finely chopped celery
4 cloves garlic, minced
8 cups (2 L) vegetable stock

2 cups (500 mL) chopped tomatoes
3 jalapeño chilies, seeded and minced
2 tsp (10 mL) sweet Hungarian paprika
1 tsp (5 mL) ground cumin
1 cup (250 mL) finely chopped cilantro
1 Tbsp (15 mL) fresh lemon juice
Salt and pepper to taste
Sour cream for garnish
Finely chopped chives for garnish (optional)

1. Soak the beans (see page 4).

2. In a large pot, heat the oil over medium heat. Add the onions, peppers, carrots, celery and garlic. Cook, stirring often, until the onion has softened.

3. Add the beans, stock, tomatoes, jalapeños, paprika and cumin. Bring to a boil.

4. Reduce the heat and simmer, partially covered, until the beans are starting to fall apart, at least 2 hours.

5. Stir in the cilantro and lemon juice. Season with salt and pepper to taste.

6. Ladle out hearty bowlfuls and top with dollops of sour cream and a sprinkling of chives.

Savory Rutabaga and Red Lentil Soup

Anne Desjardins, Consulting Chef, Montreal

Makes about 6 servings

I created this version of red lentil soup specially for Soup Sisters using ingredients that are nourishing and easy to find. Black peppercorns, turmeric and ginger are all spices with confirmed antioxidant power. This soup freezes well but don't add the cream and parsley until just before serving. So, cook a big batch, freeze some for later and enjoy the rest now!
—Anne Desjardins

2 Tbsp (30 mL) canola oil
½ cup (125 mL) finely chopped onion
1 Tbsp (15 mL) peeled and grated fresh ginger
1 clove garlic, minced
1 tsp (5 mL) turmeric
1 tsp (5 mL) finely grated orange zest
5 whole black peppercorns
1½ lb (750 g) rutabaga, peeled and cubed
1 cup (250 mL) red lentils, picked over and rinsed

1 tsp (5 mL) granulated sugar, maple syrup or honey
8 cups (2 L) water or chicken stock
¼ cup (60 mL) whipping cream (35% MF)
1 tsp (5 mL) apple cider vinegar
Salt to taste
Angostura bitters to taste (optional)
Tabasco sauce to taste
2 Tbsp (30 mL) finely chopped parsley for garnish

1. In a large pot, heat the oil over medium heat. Add the onion, ginger, garlic, turmeric, orange zest and peppercorns. Cook, stirring often, until the onion has softened.

2. Add the rutabaga, lentils and sugar. Cook, stirring often, for 3 minutes.

3. Add the water. Bring to a boil.

4. Reduce the heat and simmer, covered, until the rutabaga and lentils are tender, about 45 minutes.

5. Purée the soup until smooth. Reheat gently.

6. Add the cream and vinegar, and season with salt, Angostura (if using) and Tabasco sauce to taste.

7. Ladle into bowls and add a scattering of parsley to each.

Speedy Triple S Soup

Karen Anderson, Owner, Calgary Food Tours Inc.

Makes about 8 servings

1 Tbsp (15 mL) olive oil

1 lb (500 g) chicken or turkey sausage, cut into bite-size rounds

1 onion, finely chopped

2 cloves garlic, minced

1 tsp (5 mL) red chili flakes

½ cup (125 mL) white wine

2 cans (each 19 oz/540 mL) white cannellini beans or other canned beans, drained and rinsed

1 can (28 oz/796 mL) tomatoes with their juice

1 pkg (12 oz/375 g) frozen butternut squash or sweet potato

1 pkg (10 oz/300 g) frozen chopped spinach

1 tsp (5 mL) dried basil leaves

1 tsp (5 mL) dried oregano leaves

Salt and pepper to taste

Piece of Parmesan cheese to shave for garnish

1. In a large pot, heat the oil over medium heat. Add the sausage. Cook, stirring often, until the sausage is browned on all sides.

2. Add the onion to the pot. Cook, stirring often, until the onion has softened.

3. Add the garlic and chili flakes. Cook, stirring, until fragrant, about 1 minute.

4. Gradually add the wine, stirring to scrape up any browned bits from the bottom of the pot.

5. Add the beans, tomatoes, 2 tomato canfuls of water, the squash, spinach, basil and oregano. Bring to a boil.

6. Reduce the heat and simmer, covered, until the squash and spinach have thawed and the soup is piping hot, about 15 minutes. Season with salt and pepper to taste.

7. Ladle the soup into bowls and, with a sharp vegetable peeler, shave slivers of Parmesan over each hearty bowlful.

If you keep the right things in your pantry, fridge and freezer, you'll always be able to whip up something delicious at a moment's notice. This speedy soup—the three Ss are sausage, squash and spinach—proves my theory. It's a nutritional powerhouse and as good-looking as it is tasty. Serve on its own for a hearty lunch or with grilled cheese sandwiches for a comforting dinner.
—Karen Anderson

Split Pea Soup with Smoked Turkey and Collards

Lucy Waverman, Cookbook Author and Food Columnist

Makes about 8 servings

Smoked turkey meat is salty, so be sure to season the soup carefully. If the turkey leg is very meaty, cut off some of the meat before making the soup to reserve for another occasion (it makes great sandwiches).
—Lucy Waverman

1 Tbsp (15 mL) butter
1 cup (250 mL) chopped onions
½ cup (125 mL) peeled and diced carrot
½ cup (125 mL) diced celery
1 bunch collard greens, center ribs and stems removed, leaves cut into 1-inch (2.5 cm) strips
6 cups (1.5 L) chicken stock
1 lb (500 g) smoked turkey leg with bone
2 cups (500 mL) dried yellow split peas, picked over and rinsed

2 cups (500 mL) water
1 Tbsp (15 mL) finely chopped fresh thyme
1 bay leaf
Salt and pepper to taste
2 Tbsp (30 mL) finely chopped parsley for garnish
2 Tbsp (30 mL) extra virgin olive oil for garnish

1. In a large pot, heat the butter over medium heat. Add the onions, carrot and celery. Cook, stirring often, until the onion starts to soften.

2. Add the collard greens. Cook, stirring often, until the greens start to wilt, about 2 minutes.

3. Add the stock, smoked turkey leg, peas, water, thyme and bay leaf. Bring to a boil.

4. Reduce the heat and simmer, uncovered, until the peas are tender, about 1 hour. If the soup gets too thick, add more water.

5. Remove the turkey leg and set aside. Remove the bay leaf. Purée half of the soup until smooth.

6. Add the puréed soup back to the pot. Season with salt and pepper to taste.

7. Remove some of the turkey meat from the leg and shred it finely.

8. Ladle the soup into bowls and scatter each bowlful with some shredded turkey and parsley, plus a drizzle of extra virgin olive oil.

Turkey Meatball Soup

Naheed Nenshi, Broth Brother and Mayor of Calgary

Makes about 4 servings

Meatballs

¾ cup (185 mL) freshly grated Parmesan
   cheese
¼ cup (60 mL) grated onion
1 egg
2 Tbsp (30 mL) dried parsley leaves
Pinch of salt and pepper
1 lb (500 g) ground turkey

Soup

3 cups (750 mL) chicken or vegetable
   stock
3 cups (750 mL) water
½ cup (125 mL) thinly sliced carrot
½ cup (125 mL) chopped green onions
¼ cup (60 mL) thinly sliced celery
1 tsp (5 mL) dried thyme leaves
1 tsp (5 mL) dried basil leaves
¼ tsp (1 mL) salt
1 cup (250 mL) broken noodle-type pasta
   (vermicelli or fine egg noodles work
   best)
½ cup (125 mL) seeded and diced sweet
   red pepper

1. For the meatballs, preheat the oven to 400°F (200°C).

2. In a medium bowl, combine the Parmesan, onion, egg, parsley, salt and pepper. Add the ground turkey. Mix gently.

3. Form the turkey mixture into small balls, using about 1 Tbsp (15 mL) of the turkey mixture for each meatball.

4. Arrange the meatballs in a single layer on a greased large, rimmed baking sheet. Bake until the meatballs are no longer pink inside, about 15 minutes.

5. Meanwhile, for the soup, combine the stock and water in a large pot. Bring to a boil.

6. Add the carrot, green onions, celery, thyme, basil and salt.

7. Reduce the heat and simmer, covered, until the carrot is tender, about 10 minutes.

8. Add the meatballs, pasta and red pepper to the pot. Simmer, uncovered, until the pasta is al dente, 7 to 10 minutes. (The cooking time will be longer if you use thicker noodles.)

9. Ladle into bowls, making sure everyone gets an equal number of meatballs. Fair's fair.

Turkey Soup with Kale

Cavell Hart, Soup Sister

Makes about 4 servings

8 cups (2 L) turkey stock
1 large bunch kale, center ribs and stems removed, leaves thinly sliced
2 cups (500 mL) shredded or cubed leftover turkey meat
8 oz (250 g) yolkless medium egg noodles (see sidebar)
Salt and pepper to taste

1. In a large pot, bring the stock to a gentle simmer.

2. Add the kale, turkey meat and noodles.

3. Simmer, uncovered, until the noodles are tender, about 10 minutes. Season with salt and pepper to taste.

4. Ladle up healthy, hearty bowlfuls.

Yolkless noodles never become mushy, even when this soup is reheated several times.

Thanksgiving dinner was over. All that was left was the turkey carcass. Which meant turkey soup, of course. I wanted to keep the soup simple but also wanted to add some color and texture. Enter kale, the superhero of veggies. What flavor! Now I buy turkeys just to make this, the superhero of soups.
—Cavell Hart

Winter Tomato Soup with Blue Cheese

Rose Murray, Cookbook Author

Makes about 4 servings

2 Tbsp (30 mL) butter
1 onion, finely chopped
1 stalk celery, diced
2 cloves garlic, minced
1 tsp (5 mL) Spanish sweet smoked paprika
½ tsp (2 mL) dried oregano leaves
Pinch of cayenne
Salt and pepper to taste
4 cups (1 L) chicken stock
1 can (28 oz/796 mL) diced tomatoes with their juice
½ cup (125 mL) crumbled blue cheese
2 Tbsp (30 mL) softened cream cheese

1. In a large pot, melt the butter over medium heat. Add the onion and celery. Cook, stirring often, until the onion has softened.

2. Add the garlic and cook, stirring, for 1 minute. Remove the pot from the heat and stir in the paprika, oregano, cayenne, and salt and pepper to taste.

3. Add the stock and tomatoes. Return the pot to the heat and bring to a boil.

4. Reduce the heat and simmer, covered, for 15 minutes.

5. Purée the soup until smooth. Reheat gently.

6. Just before serving, stir together the blue cheese and cream cheese in a small bowl.

7. Ladle into bowls and top each steamy portion with a dollop of the blue-cheese mixture.

This recipe is adapted from A Taste of Canada *by Rose Murray (Whitecap, 2008).*

If you have only cans of whole tomatoes in your cupboard, chop them with scissors right in the can or pot.

Who doesn't love the comfort of a bowl of tomato soup and a grilled cheese sandwich? Here I've added cheese to the soup itself for an intriguing flavor. Use whatever blue cheese you happen to have on hand; Stilton, Gorgonzola or Canadian Bleu Ermite are all good choices. (Or you can skip the blue cheese garnish and make some grilled cheese sandwiches!)
—Rose Murray

Winter Squash Soup

Susur Lee, Celebrity Chef/Owner, Lee Restaurant, Toronto

Makes about 4 servings

2 Tbsp (30 mL) pumpkin seed oil

2 cups (500 mL) peeled, seeded and cubed butternut or Japanese kabocha squash

2 Tbsp (30 mL) finely chopped onion

1 Tbsp (15 mL) diced celery

½ tsp (2 mL) minced garlic

Pinch of grated nutmeg

3 cups (750 mL) chicken or vegetable stock or carrot juice

¼ cup (60 mL) white wine

Salt and white pepper to taste

1 Tbsp (15 mL) finely diced English cucumber for garnish

1 Tbsp (15 mL) roasted pumpkin seeds for garnish

2 tsp (10 mL) honey for garnish

Kabocha squash is a Japanese vegetable that resembles a squat green pumpkin. Its pale orange flesh is similar in texture to pumpkin but much sweeter. Look for it in specialty produce or Japanese grocery stores.

1. In a large pot, heat the oil over medium-low heat. Add the squash, onion, celery, garlic and nutmeg. Cook, stirring often, until the onion has softened.

2. Add stock and wine and bring to a boil.

3. Reduce the heat and simmer, covered, until the squash is tender, about 20 minutes.

4. Purée the soup until smooth. Reheat gently. Season with salt and pepper to taste.

5. Ladle into bowls and garnish each portion with diced cucumber, a sprinkling of pumpkin seeds and a drizzle of honey.

Yardbird's Miso Soup

Matt Abergel, Chef/Co-owner, Yardbird and Ronin, Hong Kong

Makes about 8 servings

Japanese Ingredients at a Glance

Daikon: A long, white radish about the size of a very large carrot.
Kombu: Dried, edible kelp (seaweed).
Light soy sauce: Also called fresh soy sauce, not to be confused with low-sodium soy sauce. It is a slightly paler color than regular soy sauce and has a higher salt content.
Matsutake mushrooms: Expensive dried mushrooms prized in Asian cuisines for their spicy aroma.
Miso: A thick, salty paste made by fermenting rice, barley or soy beans.
Mizuna: Also called Japanese mustard, a herb resembling arugula with a mild mustard flavor.
Yuzu: A tart citrus fruit with a grapefruit/mandarin flavor.

Mushroom Dashi

12 cups (3 L) cold water
4 oz (125 g) dried shiitake mushrooms
2 oz (60 g) dried porcini mushrooms
1 oz (30 g) dried matsutake mushrooms (see sidebar)
12-inch (30 cm) piece of kombu (see sidebar)

Soup

1½ tsp (7 mL) light soy sauce (see sidebar)

Pinch of salt
⅓ cup (80 mL) rice miso (see sidebar)
¼ cup (60 mL) barley miso
½ unpeeled daikon radish (about 5 oz/150 g), thinly sliced (see sidebar)
½ head napa cabbage, thinly sliced
1 bunch mizuna, coarsely chopped (see sidebar)
1 tsp (5 mL) finely grated yuzu zest (see sidebar)

1. For the mushroom dashi, combine the water, all the dried mushrooms and the kombu in a large pot. Let soak at room temperature overnight. (This helps to extract the most glutamate, the natural component of MSG and the essential element of umami, one of the five basic tastes.)

2. For the soup, bring the mushroom dashi to a boil. Remove the kombu.

3. Boil the dashi until it turns a deep golden brown, about 20 minutes.

4. Reduce the heat to a simmer. Remove and discard the mushrooms. Add the soy sauce and salt.

5. Put both misos in a small fine-mesh sieve. Partially immerse the sieve in the soup. Rub the misos through the sieve into the soup with the back of a spoon (This prevents the miso from becoming lumpy.)

6. Add the daikon, napa cabbage, mizuna and yuzu zest.

7. Ladle the soup into bowls and enjoy.

SPRING

A time of new beginnings, in spring we see the trees come into bud and feel the sun start to strengthen. It's also the season when our soups lighten up and we welcome more volunteers to our ranks. We work with new chapters of Soup Sisters and Broth Brothers through the winter, training volunteers and arranging for more shelters to receive our nourishing soups.

Celebrate the brand-new season by ladling up some bright and lively soups such as Avgolemono, Creole Shrimp or Spring Green Herb.

Alice's Creamed Corn and Chicken Soup

Marla Rabinovitch, Soup Sister

Makes about 4 servings

From the late '70s through the '90s, we frequented the original Home Food Inn, a Chinese restaurant in Calgary. The restaurant was where we ate the night before each of our children was born, and the first place we went to from the hospital afterward. The owner, Alice, used to bring us this soup while we decided what else we wanted. Since it's a great, fast, hearty soup for a busy family, at some point I asked Alice for the recipe, and she told me what was in it. I experimented over the years and came up with my own version.
—Marla Rabinovitch

4 cups (1 L) chicken stock
1 can (14 oz/398 mL) creamed corn
1 cup (250 mL) diced cooked chicken
1 Tbsp (15 mL) sesame oil
1 Tbsp (15 mL) soy sauce
1 tsp (5 mL) rice wine vinegar
1 to 2 Tbsp (15 to 30 mL) cornstarch (depending on how thick you like your soup)
1 tsp (5 mL) water
2 egg whites
Salt and pepper to taste

1. In a large pot, combine the stock, creamed corn, chicken, sesame oil, soy sauce and rice vinegar. Bring to a boil.

2. Reduce the heat and simmer, covered, for 20 minutes.

3. In a small bowl, stir together the cornstarch and water until smooth. Add the cornstarch mixture to the pot and simmer, stirring often, for 5 minutes.

4. In another small bowl, whisk the egg whites until frothy. Stir the egg whites into the soup. Season with salt and pepper to taste.

5. Ladle into bowls and dig in.

Avgolemono Soup
(Greek Lemon, Chicken and Rice Soup)

Roslyne Buchanan, Soup Sister

Makes about 4 servings

6 cups (1.5 L) chicken stock

1 cup (250 mL) finely chopped onion

1 cup (250 mL) diced celery

1 cup (250 mL) peeled and diced carrot

⅓ cup (80 mL) long-grain rice

1 tsp (5 mL) dried thyme leaves

2 Tbsp (30 mL) finely chopped parsley, divided

1½ cups (375 mL) diced cooked chicken

2 eggs or 3 egg yolks

Juice of 1 large lemon (about ¼ cup/ 60 mL)

1 tsp (5 mL) finely grated lemon zest

Salt and pepper to taste

6 Tbsp (90 mL) whipping cream (35% MF)

1. In a large pot, bring the chicken stock to a rolling boil.

2. Add the onion, celery, carrot, rice, thyme and 1 Tbsp (15 mL) of the parsley. Boil, uncovered, until the rice is tender, about 10 minutes.

3. Add the cooked chicken. Remove the pot from the heat and let the soup cool slightly.

4. In a medium bowl, beat together the eggs and lemon juice until frothy.

5. Whisk about ½ cup (125 mL) of the cooled liquid from the soup into the egg mixture.

6. Return the pot of soup to medium heat and heat through but don't allow it to boil.

7. Strain the egg mixture into the soup, stirring constantly to create a creamy texture.

8. Add the lemon zest and season with salt and pepper to taste.

9. Slowly stir in the cream. Ladle the soup into bowls and sprinkle with the remaining parsley.

This recipe is a great way to use up leftover roast chicken (or turkey), especially if you boil up the carcass to make the stock. You can use both the light and dark meat of the bird. Or use purchased stock and chicken from the deli.
—Roslyne Buchanan

Carrot Soup with Lemon-Tahini Dollop and Crisped Chickpeas

Deb Perelman, Cookbook Author and Blogger, smittenkitchen.com

Makes about 4 servings

2 Tbsp (30 mL) olive oil
2 lb (1 kg) carrots, peeled and diced
1 large onion, finely chopped
4 cloves garlic, peeled and smashed
½ tsp (2 mL) ground cumin
½ tsp (2 mL) table salt
¼ tsp (1 mL) ground coriander
Pinch of Aleppo pepper flakes (see sidebar) or red chili flakes
4 cups (1 L) vegetable stock

Aleppo pepper flakes are a mild, peppery seasoning, used in Mediterranean and Middle Eastern dishes, with a flavor similar to ancho chili. Za'atar is a Middle Eastern spice blend made from dried herbs, sesame seeds, dried sumac and salt.

Lemon-Tahini Dollop

3 Tbsp (45 mL) tahini paste (see page 151)
2 Tbsp (30 mL) fresh lemon juice
2 Tbsp (30 mL) water (approx.)
Pinch of salt

Toppings (optional)

2 large pitas, each cut into 8 wedges
Olive oil for brushing
Za'atar (see sidebar) or sesame seeds and sea salt to taste
Crisped chickpeas (see page 114)
2 Tbsp (30 mL) coarsely chopped parsley

1. For the soup, heat the oil in a large pot over medium heat. Add the carrots, onion, garlic, cumin, salt, coriander and pepper flakes. Cook, stirring often, until the onion begins to brown.

2. Add the stock. Bring to a boil, stirring to scrape up any browned bits from the bottom of the pot.

3. Reduce the heat and simmer, covered and stirring occasionally, until the carrots are tender, about 30 minutes.

4. For the lemon-tahini dollop, whisk together the tahini, lemon juice, 2 Tbsp (30 mL) water and salt in a small bowl until smooth and with a yogurt-like consistency. If the mixture is too thick to dollop, add a little more water.

cont'd on page 114

5. For the garnish, preheat the oven to 425°F (220°C). Arrange the pita wedges in a single layer on a large baking sheet. Brush lightly with oil. Sprinkle with za'atar or a combination of sesame seeds and sea salt. Toast the pita wedges in the oven until brown at the edges, about 5 minutes.

6. Purée the soup until smooth. Reheat gently.

7. Ladle into bowls. Dollop each portion with lemon-tahini, a sprinkle of crisped chickpeas and flourish of chopped parsley. Serve with the pita wedges.

Crisped Chickpeas

Makes 1¾ cups (435 mL)

1¾ cups (435 mL) drained canned or cooked chickpeas, patted dry on paper towels
1 Tbsp (15 mL) olive oil
½ tsp (2 mL) salt
¼ tsp (1 mL) ground cumin

1. Preheat the oven to 425°F (220°C).

2. In a medium bowl, toss together the chickpeas, oil, salt and cumin until well coated.

3. Spread out the chickpeas on a rimmed baking sheet. Roast, tossing occasionally, until they're browned and crisp, 10 to 20 minutes, depending on the size and firmness of your chickpeas.

Since I confess to finding soup a little dull, I tend to overcompensate with add-ins. Here, there are a dollop of lemon-tahini, a "crouton" of cumin-crisped chickpeas, wedges of toasted pita and a garnish of parsley. To you this might seem like overkill, in which case just use whatever you find the most interesting.
—Deb Perelman

Chef's Plantain Soup

Jacqueline-Marie Clement, Soup Sister

Makes about 4 servings

1 Tbsp (15 mL) olive oil
1 carrot, peeled and finely chopped
1 stalk celery, finely chopped
1 small onion, finely chopped
2 cloves garlic, minced
4 cups (1 L) chicken or vegetable stock (approx.)
2 green plantains, peeled and thinly sliced
1 small bunch cilantro (6 to 9 stems), roots and tough stems removed, finely chopped and divided
1 tsp (5 mL) cumin seeds
1 bay leaf
Salt and pepper to taste

1. In a large pot, heat the oil over medium heat. Add the carrot, celery, onion and garlic. Cook, stirring often, until the onion has softened.

2. Add 4 cups (1 L) stock. Bring to a boil.

3. Add the plantains, two-thirds of the cilantro, the cumin seeds, bay leaf, and salt and pepper to taste.

4. Reduce the heat and simmer, covered, until the vegetables are very tender, about 1 hour.

5. Remove the bay leaf. Purée the soup until smooth. If the soup is too thick, add a little more stock. Reheat gently.

6. Ladle into bowls and add a bright scattering of the remaining cilantro.

The "chef" of this soup's name was the surgeon at the local hospital near where I lived in Guyana. A family friend and good cook, he often served this soup when we visited. Strange as it may sound, it's possible to feel chilly in the late evening during the rainy season near the equator, and a nice hot soup is welcome. So relax, let your mind wander to the coast of Guyana, and savor this fragrant, velvety soup.
—Jacqueline-Marie Clement

Creamy Sunchoke Soup

Kyle Mortimer-Proulx, Chef, ZenKitchen

Makes about 6 servings

2 Tbsp (30 mL) olive oil

1 Spanish onion, chopped

1 leek (white part only), cut into ¼-inch (6 mm) slices

2 stalks celery, cut into ½-inch (1 cm) slices

1 cup (250 mL) white wine

1 lb (500 g) Jerusalem artichokes (sunchokes), washed, trimmed of any "eyes," cut into 1-inch (2.5 cm) pieces

4 cups (1 L) unflavored rice milk

Juice of 1 lemon

Pinch of salt

Rye croutons

This velvety soup features the underused sunchoke (aka Jerusalem artichoke), which provides a wonderful silky texture and a flavor somewhere between parsnips, cauliflower and salsify. At the restaurant I serve it with an assortment of pickled vegetables— green beans, butternut squash, cauliflower and carrots—and a handful of rye croutons. The vinegar from the pickles and the crunchy croutons add a nice dimension to the soup.
—Kyle Mortimer-Proulx

1. In a large, heavy-bottomed, nonreactive pot, heat the oil over medium heat. Add the onion. Cook, stirring often, until the onion has softened but is not brown.

2. Add the leek and cook, stirring often, for 2 minutes.

3. Add the celery and cook, stirring often, for 3 minutes, still not letting the vegetables color.

4. Add the wine and bring to a boil. Let bubble until the wine has reduced by about half.

5. Add the artichokes and cook, stirring often, for 3 to 4 minutes.

6. Add the rice milk and bring to a boil.

7. Reduce the heat and simmer, covered, until the artichokes are tender, about 45 minutes.

8. Purée the soup until smooth. Strain through a fine-mesh sieve back into the pot, pressing on the solids with a ladle. Reheat gently.

9. Juice the lemon directly into the soup and season with salt to taste. Ladle up silky, smooth bowlfuls and scatter with croutons.

Creole Shrimp Soup

Marian C. Hanna, Soup Sister

Makes about 8 servings

¼ cup (60 mL) canola oil

¼ cup (60 mL) quinoa flour

1½ cups (375 mL) finely chopped onions

1 cup (250 mL) diced celery

1 large sweet green, red or yellow pepper, seeded and diced

½ cup (125 mL) chopped green onions

2 to 4 cloves garlic, minced (according to taste)

½ lemon

2 cups (500 mL) chicken or fish stock or water

1 can (28 oz/796 mL) diced tomatoes

1 can (14 oz/398 mL) tomato sauce

1 can (5½ oz/156 mL) tomato paste

2 tsp (10 mL) Worcestershire sauce (optional)

1½ tsp (7 mL) salt

1 tsp (5 mL) pepper

½ tsp (2 mL) cayenne

2 bay leaves

Steamed rice for serving (optional)

3 lb (1.5 kg) shrimp, peeled and deveined

½ cup (125 mL) finely chopped parsley for garnish

Tabasco sauce for serving

When I was growing up in New Orleans, my grandparents owned a restaurant, and that experience taught us all to cook adventurously. The basis of this soup is the sauce picante, a spicy, flavorful tomato sauce. Many Creole-influenced recipes involve rice with some sort of spicy sauce of vegetables, beans, meats, seafood or even alligator. The spices are not only flavorful but also contribute to better circulation and a cleaner system. That's my story and I'm sticking to it.
—Marian C. Hanna

1. In a large, heavy-bottomed pot, make the roux by heating the oil over medium-high heat until it's shimmering. Add the flour. Cook, stirring constantly, until the roux is the color of peanut butter.

2. Add the onions, celery and pepper. Cook, stirring often, until the onions have softened. Reduce the heat to medium. Add the green onions and garlic. Cook, stirring often, until the vegetables have softened, about 15 minutes.

3. Finely grate the rind and squeeze the juice from the lemon half. Add both rind and juice to the pot along with the stock, tomatoes, tomato sauce, tomato paste, Worcestershire sauce (if using), salt, pepper, cayenne and bay leaves. Bring to a boil.

4. Reduce the heat and simmer, covered and stirring occasionally, for 50 minutes.

5. During the last 20 to 30 minutes of simmering time, prepare some rice (if using) to serve with the soup.

6. Remove the bay leaves. For a thicker soup, purée until smooth, or leave as is.

7. Add the shrimp. Simmer, uncovered, until the shrimp are pink and firm, about 10 minutes.

8. Ladle the soup into wide bowls, with or without rice. Scatter with parsley. Serve with Tabasco on the side.

Ginny's Libyan Soup

Ginny Glover, Soup Sister

Makes about 4 servings

¼ cup (60 mL) olive oil

1 Tbsp (15 mL) butter

½ lb (250 g) boneless lamb leg or
   shoulder, cubed

1 onion, finely chopped

5 whole cardamom pods, crushed
   (optional)

3 bay leaves

1 cinnamon stick

2 tomatoes, finely chopped

½ cup (125 mL) drained canned
   chickpeas

2 Tbsp (30 mL) tomato paste

1 Tbsp (15 mL) salt

1 tsp (5 mL) sweet Hungarian paprika

1 tsp (5 mL) pepper

1 tsp (5 mL) hararat (see page 119) or
   mixed spice

1 tsp (5 mL) turmeric

6 cups (1.5 L) boiling water, divided

½ cup (125 mL) finely chopped parsley,
   divided

½ cup (125 mL) orzo

1 Tbsp (15 mL) dried mint leaves

Lemon wedges for garnish

Mint sprigs for garnish

1. In a large pot, heat the olive oil and butter over medium-high heat. Add the lamb, onion, cardamom pods (if using), bay leaves and cinnamon stick. Cook, stirring often, until the onion has softened.

2. Add the tomatoes, chickpeas, tomato paste, salt, paprika, pepper, hararat and turmeric.

3. Reduce the heat. Cook, stirring often, until well combined.

4. Add 2 cups (500 mL) of the boiling water and 2 Tbsp (30 mL) of the parsley. Simmer, covered, until the lamb is tender, about 45 minutes.

5. Remove the bay leaves and cinnamon stick. Add the remaining boiling water and parsley, and orzo. Simmer, uncovered, until the orzo is tender, about 10 minutes.

6. Remove the pot from the heat. Add the mint, rubbing it between your palms as you add it.

7. Ladle the soup into bowls and garnish with lemon wedges and mint sprigs.

Hararat

Makes about 1 Tbsp (15 mL)

1 tsp (5 mL) ground cinnamon
1 tsp (5 mL) ground coriander
1 tsp (5 mL) ground cumin
¼ tsp (1 mL) ground allspice
¼ tsp (1 mL) red chili flakes

1. Heat a small nonstick skillet over medium-high heat.

2. Add the spices and cook, stirring constantly, until aromatic, 2 to 4 minutes. Do not brown.

3. Let the spice mixture cool completely. Scrape the spice mixture into a small airtight container. (Hararat will keep for up to 2 months.)

A few years ago, my husband and I spent almost two years living in the Libyan capital of Tripoli. Numerous variations of this soup are served almost everywhere in the city. Mine combines several recipes but preserves the essence of the traditional Libyan soup. It's easy, hearty and very adaptable.
—Ginny Glover

Leek and Yukon Gold Potato Soup

Anna March, Chef, The Urban Element, Ottawa

Use only the white part of the leeks. The fiber in the darker green part never really breaks down and will give a coarse consistency to the soup. Save the trimmings and use to make a vegetable stock (see page 10).

This soup warms both the belly and the soul and is the number one most requested appetizer in our corporate teambuilding classes. It works well all year round, but is especially tasty when tender spring leeks become available. If gluten isn't a problem, crowning this soup with buttery, homemade croutons would definitely add a decadent touch.
—Anna March

Makes about 8 servings

2 Tbsp (30 mL) canola oil
8 oz (250 g) double-smoked bacon, chopped
2 onions, thinly sliced
2 leeks (white parts only), thinly sliced
2 cloves garlic, minced
1 cup (250 mL) white wine
6 cups (1.5 L) chicken stock

3 medium Yukon Gold potatoes, peeled and diced
1 cup (250 mL) whipping cream (35% MF)
2 Tbsp (30 mL) butter
3 sprigs thyme
1 bay leaf
Salt and pepper to taste
Water as required

1. In a large pot, heat the oil over medium heat. Add the bacon. Cook, stirring often, until crisp. Transfer to paper towels to drain.

2. Add the onions, leeks and garlic to the pot. Cook, stirring often, until the onions have softened but are not brown.

3. Add the wine and bring to a boil, stirring to scrape up any browned bits from the bottom of the pot.

4. Add the stock, potatoes, cream, butter, thyme, bay leaf, and salt and pepper to taste. Bring to a boil. Add water, if necessary, so vegetables are completely covered.

5. Reduce the heat and simmer, covered and stirring often to make sure the soup doesn't scorch, until the vegetables are very tender, about 30 minutes. Remove the thyme stems and bay leaf.

6. Purée the soup until smooth. For a super-smooth soup, strain through a fine-mesh sieve into a clean pot.

7. Add the reserved bacon and reheat the soup gently. Season with salt and pepper to taste and add more water if the soup is too thick; it should be pourable but not watery.

8. Ladle out steaming bowlfuls and enjoy.

Lentil Soup Infused with Fried Garlic and Curry Leaves

Shefali Somani, Soup Sister and Owner, Shef's Fiery Kitchen

Makes about 6 servings

3 cups (750 mL) red lentils (masoor dal)
8 cups (2 L) water
¾ tsp (4 mL) turmeric
2 tsp (10 mL) salt
2 cups (500 mL) finely chopped cilantro
2 bunches spinach, washed
1½ cups (375 mL) chopped tomatoes
3 Tbsp (45 mL) thin slivers of fresh ginger
4 tsp (20 mL) green chili paste (see recipe at right)
2 Tbsp (30 mL) vegetable oil
12 to 14 cloves garlic, sliced
20 to 25 curry leaves (see sidebar)
Steamed rice to serve (optional)

Green Chili Paste

Makes about ½ cup (125 mL)

1 cup (250 mL) lightly packed cilantro leaves
4 green chilies, coarsely chopped
1 tsp (5 mL) fresh lemon juice
Pinch of salt

In a mini chopper or mortar and pestle, blend or grind the cilantro, chilies, lemon juice and salt until a paste forms. (The paste will keep in an airtight container in the fridge for up to 2 weeks.)

Curry leaves are from a plant native to South Asia. They have a pungent curry fragrance and appear often in South Asian recipes. Look for fresh or dried curry leaves in your local Indian or Pakistani grocery store.

1. Rinse the lentils in cold water until the water runs fairly clear. Drain well.

2. In a large pot, combine the lentils and 8 cups (2 L) water. Let stand for 10 minutes.

3. Bring the lentils and water to a boil. With a large metal spoon, skim off any froth from the surface. Reduce the heat and stir in the turmeric. Simmer, partially covered, until the lentils are tender, about 20 minutes. Stir in the salt.

4. Purée the lentils until fairly smooth.

5. Bring the puréed lentils to a gentle boil. Add the cilantro, spinach, tomatoes, ginger and chili paste. Reduce the heat and simmer, covered, for 10 minutes.

6. Meanwhile, heat the oil in a small skillet over medium heat. Add the garlic. Cook, stirring often, for 1 minute.

7. Add the curry leaves. Cook, stirring often, until the garlic is golden, 2 to 3 minutes.

8. Remove the pot from the heat. Stir in the garlic mixture. Let the soup stand, covered, for 5 minutes.

9. Ladle the soup into bowls or over rice (if using), and tuck in.

Mexican Lime Soup with Chicken

Linda Green, Soup Sister

Mexican oregano has a stronger flavor than Mediterranean oregano. Look for it in Latin grocery stores, or substitute regular dried oregano.

Makes about 4 servings

3 to 4 limes, divided	3 cups (750 mL) chicken stock
2 bone-in, skin-on chicken breasts (each about 10 oz/300 g)	3 cups (750 mL) water
1 tsp (5 mL) salt	1½ tsp (7 mL) dried Mexican oregano leaves (see sidebar) or regular dried oregano leaves
½ tsp (2 mL) pepper	1 avocado, pitted, peeled and sliced, to serve
1 Tbsp (15 mL) olive oil	
1 large onion, finely chopped	2 oz (60 g) queso fresco (see sidebar) or feta cheese, crumbled, to serve
5 to 6 cloves garlic, minced (according to taste)	
1 jalapeño chili, seeded and minced	

I make this hearty chicken soup often during winters in Mexico. The chickens at the market there are so fresh they were running around just hours earlier! Queso fresco (fresh cheese) is readily available in Mexico. Latin grocery stores or good cheese stores may carry it in Canada, or you can always substitute a mild feta. If I'm in a hurry, I sometimes skip browning the chicken and just let it poach in the broth.
—Linda Green

1. Cut 1 lime into wedges and set aside for serving. Juice the remaining limes to yield ¼ cup (60 mL) of juice. Set aside.

2. Sprinkle the chicken breasts with the salt and pepper. In a large pot, heat the oil over medium heat. Add the chicken, skin side down, and cook until browned, about 5 minutes. Transfer to a plate.

3. Add the onion to the pot. Cook, stirring often, until the onion has softened.

4. Add the garlic and jalapeño. Cook, stirring, until fragrant, about 1 minute.

5. Add the stock, water, reserved lime juice and the oregano. Return the chicken to the pot. Bring to a boil, using a large metal spoon to skim off any foam that rises to the surface.

6. Reduce the heat and simmer, partially covered, until the chicken is no longer pink when pierced with the tip of a sharp knife near the bone, about 30 minutes.

7. Transfer the chicken to a board, cover, and let cool slightly. Keep the soup at a simmer.

8. When the chicken is cool enough to handle, remove and discard the skin and bones. Shred the chicken into bite-size pieces.

9. Stir the chicken back into the soup. Season with salt and pepper to taste.

10. Put the avocado, cheese and lime wedges in separate small bowls. Ladle the soup into soup bowls and serve with the avocado, cheese and lime wedges alongside. *¡ Buen provecho !*

Mushroom Soup with Naked Oats

Paula Roy, Soup Sister

Makes about 4 servings

1/3 cup (80 mL) butter, divided

1 onion, finely chopped

1 stalk celery, diced

1 carrot, peeled and coarsely shredded

1/3 cup (80 mL) Cavena Nuda ("naked oats"; see sidebar)

8 oz (250 g) cremini or white button mushrooms, thinly sliced

4 cups (1 L) chicken or vegetable stock

1/4 cup (60 mL) all-purpose flour

1 cup (250 mL) milk

1 tsp (5 mL) dried thyme leaves

1/4 tsp (1 mL) pepper

Salt to taste

Cavena Nuda is an amazing variety of hull-less oats (naked, get it?) developed in Manitoba. Also called Rice of the Prairies, this grain looks and cooks like brown rice, but has a far more substantial nutritional profile: high in fiber and protein, a good source of iron, and gluten free. Its chewy texture and slightly nutty flavor make it a great addition to soups and stews. Look for it at your natural food store, or substitute pot barley.
—Paula Roy

1. In a large pot, heat 2 Tbsp (30 mL) of the butter over medium-low heat. Add the onion, celery and carrot. Cook, stirring often, until the onion starts to soften.

2. Add the Cavena Nuda. Cook, stirring to coat the grains with butter.

3. Add the mushrooms and increase the heat to medium-high. Cook, stirring often, until the mushrooms start to brown.

4. Add the stock. Bring to a boil.

5. Reduce the heat and simmer, covered, until the vegetables and Cavena Nuda are tender, about 40 minutes.

6. Meanwhile, melt the remaining butter in a small saucepan.

7. Add the flour. Cook, stirring constantly, until the flour smells a bit like cookies baking.

8. Slowly add the milk, whisking constantly, until a smooth sauce forms.

9. Add the thyme and pepper. Cook over medium heat, whisking often, until the sauce is smooth and thick.

10. After the soup has simmered for 40 minutes, add the sauce. Stir thoroughly and season with salt and more pepper to taste.

11. Ladle into bowls and serve with crusty bread to mop up every scrap from the bowl. You won't want to waste a drop.

My Auntie Bev's Wonderful Mushroom Soup

Lynne Oreck-Wener, Soup Sister

Makes about 6 servings

2 Tbsp (30 mL) olive oil
2 Tbsp (30 mL) butter
1 lb (500 g) your favorite mushrooms, thinly sliced
1 onion, finely chopped
2 cloves garlic, minced
3 Tbsp (45 mL) tomato paste
3 cups (750 mL) chicken or vegetable stock
3 egg yolks
½ cup (125 mL) white vermouth
¼ cup (60 mL) freshly grated Parmesan cheese
Salt and pepper to taste

1. In a large pot, heat the oil and butter over medium heat. Add the mushrooms, onion and garlic. Cook, stirring often, until the onion has softened.

2. Stir in the tomato paste (the mixture will look awful, but don't worry).

3. Add the stock. Bring to a boil.

4. Reduce the heat and simmer, covered, until the mushrooms and onion are tender, 15 to 20 minutes.

5. In a small bowl, beat the egg yolks with a fork. Beat in some of the hot soup.

6. Add the egg-yolk mixture back to the pot and heat through (do not boil).

7. Stir in the vermouth, Parmesan, and salt and pepper to taste.

8. Ladle up elegant bowlfuls and enjoy.

My Auntie Bev was an amazing cook. This is one of her recipes that our family loved. My mom used it for all her special dinner parties. Back in the day—my mom is now 89—there wasn't much choice in Winnipeg when it came to mushrooms, so feel free to use any you like in this soup.
—Lynne Oreck-Wener

Paella Chowder

Shelley Adams, Cookbook Author

Makes about 4 servings

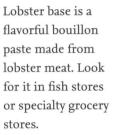

Lobster base is a flavorful bouillon paste made from lobster meat. Look for it in fish stores or specialty grocery stores.

Studded with spicy sausage, shrimp and saffron-hued rice, this intriguing soup will remind you of the traditional flavors of Spanish paella. Filling and flavorful, this is a perfect year-round soup.
—Shelley Adams

2 Tbsp (30 mL) olive oil

1 onion, finely chopped

2 stalks celery, diced

1 carrot, peeled and diced

1 tsp (5 mL) lobster base (see sidebar) or tomato paste

4 cups (1 L) chicken stock

1 cup (250 mL) white wine or dry sherry

¼ cup (60 mL) long grain rice

½ tsp (2 mL) saffron threads, crumbled

2 smoked Italian sausages, cooked and thinly sliced on the diagonal

1 boneless, skinless chicken breast, cooked and sliced

1 cup (250 mL) frozen peas, thawed

½ cup (125 mL) whipping cream (35% MF)

¾ lb (375 g) raw shrimp, shelled and deveined

2 Tbsp (30 mL) finely chopped green onions for garnish

1. In a large pot, heat the oil over medium heat. Add the onion, celery and carrot. Cook, stirring often, until the onion has softened.

2. Stir in the lobster base (if using).

3. Add the stock, wine, rice and saffron. Bring to a boil.

4. Reduce the heat and simmer, covered, until the vegetables and rice are tender, about 20 minutes.

5. Purée the soup until smooth.

6. Add the sausages, chicken, peas and cream. Cook over medium heat, stirring often, for 10 minutes.

7. Add the shrimp. Cook, stirring occasionally, until the shrimp are pink, about 3 minutes.

8. Ladle up chunky bowlfuls and scatter with green onions.

Rapini Soup

Anna Giordano, Soup Sister

Makes about 6 servings

⅓ cup (80 mL) olive oil
3 stalks celery, diced
2 carrots, peeled and diced
1 onion, finely chopped
2 cloves garlic, minced
1 tsp (5 mL) red chili flakes (or to taste)
8 cups (2 L) chicken or vegetable stock
3 cups (750 mL) coarsely chopped rapini
1 russet potato, peeled and diced
Salt and pepper to taste
1 cup (250 mL) freshly grated Parmesan or Romano cheese

I grew up eating sautéed rapini with sausages or pasta with rapini and loved its slightly bitter taste. I think it makes an interesting addition to a soup. For a heartier meal, add some sliced cooked Italian sausage to the soup.
—Anna Giordano

1. In a large pot, heat the oil over medium heat. Add the celery, carrots, onion, garlic and chili flakes. Cook, stirring often, until the carrots start to soften.

2. Add the stock, rapini and potato. Bring to a boil.

3. Reduce the heat and simmer until the rapini is wilted and the potato is tender, about 15 minutes. Season with salt and pepper to taste.

4. Ladle into bowls and sprinkle generously with cheese.

Salmon and Soba Miso Soup

Lisa Ahier, Chef/Owner, Sobo, Tofino, B.C., and Cookbook Author

Makes about 6 servings

Dashi Broth

16 cups (4 L) water

2 strips (each about 4 x 4 inches/
   10 x 10 cm) kombu (see page 106)

2 cups (500 mL) bonito flakes (see
   sidebar)

Soup

16 cups (4 L) dashi broth (see above)

¼ cup (60 mL) soy sauce

¼ cup (60 mL) light miso paste

12 oz (375 g) soba noodles

¼ cup (60 mL) canola oil, divided

8 oz (250 g) shiitake mushrooms, sliced
   and stems removed

1 lb (500 g) skinless, boneless wild
   salmon, cut into 2-inch (5 cm) pieces

1 Tbsp (15 mL) salt

1 cup (250 mL) diced firm or smoked tofu

¼ cup (60 mL) thinly sliced green onions

¼ cup (60 mL) finely chopped cilantro

Bonito flakes are flakes of dried, fermented and smoked tuna. Look for bonito in Asian grocery stores.

When I moved to Tofino in 2000, I was amazed at the quality of fish. I started experimenting with Asian ingredients, and this became one of our go-to soups at home—healthy, satisfying and quick to prepare. The kombu and bonito flakes can be tricky to find, so I always buy extra as they keep well. If you can't find miso paste, instant miso broth will work. To make this soup with vegetable stock instead of dashi, add a little more soy sauce.
—Lisa Ahier

1. For the dashi broth, combine the water and kombu in a large pot. Bring to a boil and add the bonito flakes.

2. Remove the pot from the heat. Cover and let steep until the bonito flakes sink to the bottom of the pot, about 20 minutes. Strain the broth, discarding the bonito flakes and kombu.

3. For the soup, bring the broth almost to a boil in a large pot. Remove from the heat. Add the soy sauce, then whisk in the miso paste.

4. Meanwhile, cook the noodles according to the directions on the package. Drain, then rinse briefly in cool water to prevent the noodles from sticking together.

5. In a large skillet, heat 2 Tbsp (30 mL) of the oil over high heat. Add the mushrooms. Cook, stirring often, until the mushrooms have softened but are not brown. Remove from the skillet and set aside.

6. Reduce the heat to medium-high and add the remaining oil to the skillet. Season the salmon with the salt and add to the skillet. Cook, turning gently, until the salmon is golden on the outside but still pink in the center, 4 to 5 minutes.

7. Divide the salmon, shiitakes, noodles, tofu, green onions and cilantro among wide soup bowls. Ladle some of the hot miso broth into each bowl. Pour the remaining miso broth into a pitcher (I use a teapot) and put it on the table so everyone can add more broth to their bowls if they wish.

Simply Chicken Soup

Amy Nyhof, Soup Sister

Makes about 8 servings

1 Tbsp (15 mL) olive oil

8 oz (250 g) cremini or white button mushrooms, sliced (see sidebar)

1 large onion, coarsely chopped

2 Tbsp (30 mL) finely chopped garlic

16 cups (4 L) water

3½ to 4 lb (1.75 to 2 kg) whole chicken

1 Tbsp (15 mL) salt

1 bay leaf

1 cup (250 mL) wild rice blend

⅓ cup (80 mL) chopped parsley

Pepper to taste

Crackers to serve

Cremini mushrooms give this soup an earthier flavor, white mushrooms a milder one.

Recipes with long lists of ingredients intimidate me. This is probably the easiest made-from-scratch soup you'll ever try, containing basic, easy-to-find items. Best of all, it's a soup that eats like a meal!
—Amy Nyhof

1. In a large pot, heat the oil over medium-high heat. Add the mushrooms, onion and garlic. Cook, stirring often, until the onion has softened.

2. Add the water, chicken, salt and bay leaf. Bring to a boil.

3. Add the rice blend. Reduce the heat and simmer, covered, until the chicken is no longer pink inside, 45 to 60 minutes. Using a large metal spoon, occasionally skim off any fat that rises to the surface.

4. Remove the chicken from the pot and put in a colander set over a bowl. Remove the bay leaf from the broth.

5. When the chicken is cool enough to handle, remove the meat and shred it coarsely, discarding the skin and bones.

6. Return the chicken meat to the pot. Stir in the parsley. Season with more salt and pepper to taste.

7. Ladle the soup into bowls, serve with crackers and tuck in.

Smoky Trout Chowder

Signe Langford, Food Writer

Makes about 6 servings

*I love this comforting
soup for so many
reasons: it's easy to
make, not overly
creamy, subtly
smoky and made
with sustainable
trout. For this recipe,
choose a white wine
good enough to serve
with the soup—a
lightly oaked, cool-
climate Chardonnay,
perhaps—then invest
in two bottles. Serve
the soup with fresh,
crusty country bread.
—Signe Langford*

4 large yellow-fleshed potatoes, scrubbed (not peeled), divided

4½ cups (1.12 L) chicken or fish stock, divided

1 Tbsp (15 mL) butter

2 leeks (white parts only), thinly sliced

1 large stalk celery, finely diced

1 small carrot, peeled and finely diced

1 tsp (5 mL) dried thyme

1 tsp (5 mL) Spanish sweet smoked paprika

1 tsp (5 mL) white pepper

½ cup (125 mL) medium sherry

½ cup (125 mL) white wine

1½ cups (375 mL) whipping cream (35% MF)

½ cup (125 mL) coarsely chopped boneless, skinless smoked trout

12 oz (375 mL) boneless, skinless fresh trout fillets, cut into 3-inch (8 cm) pieces

Sea salt to taste

Sour cream or crème fraîche (see page 182) for garnish

Chopped fresh chives for garnish

Additional Spanish sweet smoked paprika for garnish

1. Cut 2 of the potatoes into 1-inch (2.5 cm) dice. Set aside. Chop the remaining potatoes coarsely.

2. In a large saucepan, combine the coarsely chopped potatoes and 1½ cups (375 mL) of the stock. Bring to a boil. Reduce the heat and simmer, covered, until the potatoes are falling apart and are soft enough to mash easily, about 15 minutes. Do not drain.

3. Using a potato masher, mash the potatoes and the liquid right in the saucepan. Cover and set aside.

4. In a large, heavy-bottomed pot, melt the butter over low heat. Add the reserved diced potatoes, leeks, celery, carrot, thyme, paprika and pepper. Cook, stirring often to prevent sticking, until the leeks have softened.

5. Add the sherry and wine and bring to a boil. Boil until the aroma is almost gone, 1 to 2 minutes.

6. Stir in the remaining stock, the mashed potatoes, cream and smoked trout. Bring to a gentle simmer. Cook, uncovered and stirring often, for 15 minutes.

7. Add the fresh trout and simmer, uncovered, for 5 minutes, stirring gently and being careful not to break up the pieces of fresh trout. Season with salt to taste.

8. Ladle into bowls, making sure everyone gets some fresh trout. Top each bowl with a dollop of sour cream or crème fraîche, a sprinkling of chives and a dusting of smoked paprika.

Smashing Oyster Soup

Jennifer Schell, Soup Sister, Cookbook Author and Editor of
Food & Wine Trails Magazine

Makes about 4 servings

4 slices bacon
2 Tbsp (30 mL) butter
1 cup (250 mL) minced onion or shallots
1 cup (250 mL) minced celery
3 cups (750 mL) half-and-half cream (10% MF)
2 cups (500 mL) homogenized milk (3.25% MF)
24 fresh oysters, shucked
Salt and pepper to taste
Chopped chives and Spanish sweet smoked paprika for garnish

1. In a large skillet, cook the bacon over medium heat until it's crispy. Transfer to paper towels to drain. Crumble the bacon into small pieces. Set aside.

2. In the same skillet, melt the butter over medium heat. Add the onion and celery. Cook, stirring often, until the onion has softened. Set aside.

3. In a large pot over medium-high heat, combine the cream and milk.

4. Add the onion mixture and bacon to the pot. Heat, stirring continuously, until the soup is almost boiling (do not boil).

5. Add the oysters and their liquid. Cook without boiling, stirring gently, just until the oysters curl at the edges.

6. Remove the pot from the heat. Season with salt and pepper to taste.

7. Ladle the soup into bowls, dividing the oysters evenly. Add a flourish of chopped chives and smoked paprika to each bowl.

How should an oyster taste? "Like kissing the sea on the lips," according to the French poet Léon-Paul Fargue.

Not quite the farm recipe you would expect from an Okanagan orchard girl, but this easy soup is a perfect celebration of ocean-to-table living. If you don't live near the sea like I do, your local fishmonger will always have containers of preshucked oysters at the ready. This soup is perfect served for a rustic lunch with a big piece of crusty bread, but is elegant enough to make a beautiful starter for a special dinner.
—Jennifer Schell

Sorrel and Fennel Soup

Michael Allemeier, Chef and Culinary Instructor, SAIT (Southern Alberta Institute of Technology), Calgary

Makes about 6 servings

2 Tbsp (30 mL) canola oil
1 large onion, finely chopped
1 fennel bulb, diced
1 russet potato, peeled and diced
8 cups (2 L) chicken or vegetable stock
8 cups (2 L) lightly packed, washed sorrel leaves (about 40 leaves; see sidebar)
Salt to taste
Sorrel leaves or other herbs for garnish

1. In a large pot, heat the oil over medium heat. Add the onion and fennel. Cook, stirring often, until the onion has softened and is just starting to color.

2. Add the potato and cook, stirring, for 1 minute.

3. Add the stock and bring to a simmer.

4. Reduce the heat and simmer, covered, until the fennel is very tender, about 30 minutes.

5. Add the sorrel leaves and remove the pot from the heat.

6. Purée the soup until smooth. Reheat gently. Season with salt to taste. It's best not to cook or heat this soup for too long, as doing so will dull the flavor and the color.

7. Ladle up steaming bowlfuls and enjoy!

Sorrel is a hardy perennial herb that's been used in many cuisines for centuries. Its long, slender leaves look similar to spinach but have a tangy, slightly acidic flavor. Look for sorrel in the spring at farmers' markets or in specialty produce stores.

Spring Green Herb Soup

Dahlia Haas, Chef/Owner, All Seasons Cooking, Beverly Hills, USA

Makes about 6 servings

This recipe is a favorite on any cool spring night both at home in Los Angeles and on holiday in Hawaii, where our family spends many wonderful times together in the kitchen cooking, eating and sharing. Being in the kitchen grounds me and I love to cook, even on vacation, which is when I seem to gain the most inspiration.
—Dahlia Haas

2 Tbsp (30 mL) coconut oil
2 cups (500 mL) thinly shredded Swiss chard leaves or beet greens
1½ cups (375 mL) finely diced celery
1½ cups (375 mL) finely chopped leek (white parts only)
1½ cups (375 mL) finely diced fennel
4 cloves garlic, thinly sliced
½ tsp (2 mL) red chili flakes
2 cups (500 mL) trimmed and thinly sliced asparagus
1½ cups (375 mL) fresh peas
6 cups (1.5 L) vegetable stock
⅓ cup (80 mL) finely chopped fresh basil
⅓ cup (80 mL) finely chopped chives
⅓ cup (80 mL) finely chopped fresh dill
2 cups (500 mL) lightly packed baby spinach
Salt and white pepper to taste
Fresh basil leaves for garnish

1. In a large pot, heat the oil over medium-low heat. Add the Swiss chard, celery, leek, fennel, garlic and chili flakes. Cook, stirring often, until the vegetables have softened.

2. Add the asparagus and peas, stirring to coat with the leek mixture.

3. Add the stock. Bring to a boil.

4. Reduce the heat and simmer, uncovered, until the vegetables are tender, 20 to 25 minutes.

5. Purée 2 cups (500 mL) of the soup, with the basil, chives and dill, until smooth.

6. Return the puréed soup to the pot. Add the spinach. Reheat gently until the spinach just wilts. Season with salt and pepper to taste.

7. Ladle into bowls, garnish with basil leaves and enjoy a taste of spring.

Stinging Nettle Soup

Danielle Bouch, Soup Sister and Blogger, foodforarchitects.wordpress.com

Makes about 4 servings

2 Tbsp (30 mL) olive oil

1 onion, finely chopped

1 stalk celery, diced

8 cups (2 L) chicken or vegetable stock

3 medium potatoes, peeled and diced (about 1½ lb/750 g)

¼ tsp (1 mL) dried thyme leaves

⅛ tsp (0.5 mL) grated nutmeg

1 bay leaf

6 cups (1.5 L) lightly packed stinging nettles (young leaves and stems only; see sidebar)

6 green onions (green part only), coarsely chopped

Salt and pepper to taste

½ cup (125 mL) plain yogurt, sour cream or crème fraîche (see page 182)

¼ cup (60 mL) hulled sunflower seeds (optional)

1. In a large pot, heat the oil over medium heat. Add the onion and celery. Cook, stirring often, until the onion has softened.

2. Add the stock, potatoes, thyme, nutmeg and bay leaf. Bring to a boil.

3. Reduce the heat and simmer, uncovered, until the potatoes are tender, 15 to 25 minutes.

4. Add the stinging nettles and green onions. (Be sure to wear gloves or use tongs when handling the stinging nettles.)

5. Simmer, stirring to submerge the nettles in the hot liquid, just until the nettles turn bright green, 30 seconds to 1 minute.

6. Remove the pot from the heat. Remove the bay leaf.

7. Purée the soup until smooth. Reheat gently. Season with salt and pepper to taste.

8. Ladle up vivid green bowlfuls. Swirl yogurt into each bowl and sprinkle with sunflower seeds (if using).

Uncooked stinging nettles will sting you, so be sure to wear gloves when handling them. For best flavor, harvest only the top section of the plant, containing the first four leaves. When foraging for any wild plants, make sure you have positively identified what you are gathering. Forage only in areas free from pesticides and herbicides where you have permission to collect plants.

This forager's soup is a wonderful introduction to wild greens. Stinging nettles have a bright flavor that's somewhere between spinach and kale, with a mild, peppery note. They're one of the first signs of spring, and the deep emerald color of this soup is welcome after a long, dark winter.
—Danielle Bouch

Sunchoke Soup with Sunchoke Chips

Jamie Kennedy, Chef/Owner, Jamie Kennedy Kitchens, Toronto

Makes about 4 servings

Soup
⅓ cup (80 mL) butter

1 onion, finely chopped

10 oz (300 g) Jerusalem artichokes (sunchokes), peeled and diced

6 cups (1.5 L) strong chicken stock

Salt and pepper to taste

Sunchoke Chips
Sunflower oil for deep-frying

1 Jerusalem artichoke (sunchoke), peeled and very thinly sliced

Salt to taste

1. For the soup, melt the butter in a large, nonreactive pot over medium heat. Add the onion and artichokes. Cook, stirring often, until the onion has softened.

2. Add the stock and salt and pepper to taste. Bring to a boil.

3. Reduce the heat and simmer for 30 minutes.

4. Meanwhile, for the sunchoke chips, pour the oil into a large, deep saucepan to a depth of 3 inches (8 cm). Heat to 275°F (135°C).

5. Fry the sliced artichoke until golden brown and crispy.

6. With a slotted spoon, transfer to paper towels to drain. Sprinkle with salt.

7. Purée the soup until smooth. Reheat gently. Season with salt and pepper to taste.

8. Ladle the soup into bowls and garnish each portion with a crunchy scattering of sunchoke chips.

For the skinniest chips, slice the Jerusalem artichoke on a mandoline slicer.

Thai Red Lentil Soup with Chili Oil

Yotam Ottolenghi, Chef, Restaurant Owner and Cookbook Author

Makes about 4 servings

Chili Oil

¾ cup (185 mL) sunflower oil, divided

1 large shallot, coarsely chopped

1 small clove garlic, coarsely chopped

2 tsp (10 mL) curry powder

1 tsp (5 mL) peeled and coarsely chopped fresh ginger

½ red chili, seeded and coarsely chopped

½ whole star anise

1 tsp (5 mL) tomato paste

Finely grated zest of ½ small lemon

Soup

4 oz (125 g) sugar snap peas

3 Tbsp (45 mL) sunflower oil

1 onion, thinly sliced

1½ Tbsp (22 mL) Thai red curry paste

4 cups (1 L) water

1 cup (250 mL) red lentils, picked over and rinsed

2 stalks lemongrass, trimmed and gently bashed with a rolling pin

4 kaffir lime leaves (see sidebar)

1 cup (250 mL) unsweetened coconut milk

Juice of 1 lime

1½ Tbsp (22 mL) soy sauce

½ tsp (2 mL) salt

¼ cup (60 mL) lightly packed cilantro leaves, coarsely chopped

Kaffir lime leaves are glossy and dark green with an intense lime flavor and aroma. Look for fresh leaves in the produce section of any large Asian supermarket. The leaves can be frozen almost indefinitely and used straight from the freezer.

1. For the chili oil, heat 2 Tbsp (30 mL) of the oil in a small saucepan over low heat. Add the shallot, garlic, curry powder, ginger, chili and star anise. Cook, stirring often, until the shallot has softened.

2. Add the tomato paste and cook, stirring, for 2 minutes.

3. Stir in the remaining oil and the lemon zest. Bring to a simmer, then simmer very gently, uncovered, for 30 minutes. Let cool, then line a fine-mesh sieve with cheesecloth and strain the mixture, discarding the flavorings. Set aside.

4. For the soup, cook the sugar snap peas in a small saucepan of boiling water for 90 seconds. Drain, refresh under cold water, then spread out on a clean towel to dry. Cut the sugar snaps diagonally into very thin slices and set aside.

cont'd on page 142

This soup is fresh, creamy and loaded with flavor. If you like your soup totally smooth, omit the sugar snaps. The chili oil recipe makes more than you'll need but it keeps well in a sealed jar in the fridge for up to a month. Add it to any recipe that needs a spicy kick.
—Yotam Ottolenghi

5. In a large pot, heat the oil over low heat. Add the onion. Cook, covered and stirring occasionally, until the onion is completely soft and sweet, 10 to 15 minutes.

6. Stir in the curry paste and cook, stirring, for 1 minute.

7. Add the water, lentils, lemongrass and lime leaves. Bring to a boil.

8. Reduce the heat and simmer, covered, until the lentils are completely soft, about 15 minutes. Remove the lemongrass and lime leaves.

9. Purée the soup until smooth. Stir in the coconut milk, lime juice, soy sauce and salt. Reheat gently and, once the soup is almost boiling, add the sugar snaps.

10. Ladle the hot soup into bowls. Add a scattering of cilantro and finish with ½ tsp (2 mL) of the chili oil drizzled over each portion.

Thai-Style Chicken Soup

Linda Keryluk, Soup Sister

Makes about 4 servings

1 lemon

1 lime

4 cups (1 L) chicken stock

2 Tbsp (30 mL) peeled and thinly sliced
fresh ginger

2 stalks lemongrass

1 lb (500 g) boneless, skinless chicken,
cut into bite-size pieces

2 cans (each 14 oz/398 mL) unsweetened
coconut milk

2 Tbsp (30 mL) granulated sugar

1 Tbsp (15 mL) soy sauce

1 tsp (5 mL) red chili flakes

3 cups (750 mL) sliced mushrooms

1 large sweet red pepper, seeded and cut
into thin strips

2 green onions, thinly sliced

¼ cup (60 mL) finely chopped fresh Thai
or regular basil

Sweet chili sauce (optional)

*This recipe was
given to me by a co-
worker at Options
Community Services
in Surrey, B.C. It's one
of my favorite soups
because, although it
may seem to contain
a lot of ingredients,
it's easy to make and
everyone loves it. Any
time you can make
people feel special, it's
worth it.*
—Linda Keryluk

1. Finely grate the zest from the lemon and the lime. Set the lemon and lime aside.

2. In a large pot, combine the lemon and lime zest, stock, ginger and lemongrass.
Bring to a simmer over medium heat.

3. Add the chicken, coconut milk, sugar, soy sauce and chili flakes. Squeeze 1 Tbsp
(15 mL) of juice from both the lemon and the lime into the pot. Bring to a boil.

4. Reduce the heat and simmer, covered, until the chicken is no longer pink inside,
about 10 minutes.

5. Add the mushrooms and red pepper. Simmer, covered, until the mushrooms are
tender, about 10 minutes.

6. Remove the lemongrass. Stir in the green onions and basil. Taste the soup and, if it's
too sour, add a little sweet chili sauce.

7. Ladle the soup into bowls and enjoy a taste of Thai.

Tomato, Herb and Parmesan Tortellini Soup

Debbie Pollard, Soup Sister

Makes about 6 servings

This filling soup is great for dinner on a cool spring day. I took inspiration from a few of my favorite soups and combined them to create this recipe. Feel free to add more basil and oregano, if you like, just before serving.
—Debbie Pollard

2 Tbsp (30 mL) plus ½ cup (125 mL) butter, divided
1 cup (250 mL) finely chopped sweet onion
1 cup (250 mL) diced celery
1 cup (250 mL) peeled and shredded carrot
4 cups (1 L) vegetable stock
1 can (28 oz/796 mL) diced tomatoes
1 Tbsp (15 mL) finely chopped fresh oregano

1 Tbsp (15 mL) finely chopped fresh basil
1 bay leaf
½ cup (125 mL) all-purpose flour
2 cups (500 mL) fresh cheese tortellini
1½ cups (375 mL) half-and-half cream (10% MF)
1 cup (250 mL) freshly grated Parmesan cheese
½ cup (125 mL) water
Salt and pepper to taste

1. In a large pot, heat 2 Tbsp (30 mL) of the butter over medium heat. Add the onion, celery and carrot. Cook, stirring often, until the vegetables start to soften.

2. Add the stock, tomatoes, oregano, basil and bay leaf. Bring to a boil.

3. Reduce the heat and simmer, partially covered, until the vegetables are tender, about 30 minutes. Remove the bay leaf.

4. Meanwhile, heat the remaining butter in a medium saucepan over low heat. Add the flour. Cook, stirring constantly, for 5 minutes. Slowly stir in 1 cup (250 mL) of the hot soup. When the mixture is smooth, add another 3 cups (750 mL) of the soup, stirring until well combined.

5. Add the flour mixture to the pot of soup, stirring to combine.

6. Add the tortellini, cream, Parmesan and water to the pot. Season with salt and pepper to taste.

7. Bring the soup to a simmer, stirring constantly. Simmer, uncovered and stirring occasionally, until the tortellini is tender, 10 to 15 minutes.

8. Ladle up hearty pasta-filled bowlfuls.

Tom Yum Soup

Sharon Hapton, Founder, Soup Sisters and Broth Brothers

A Taste of Thai
Check out the Asian aisle in your supermarket for these Thai essentials.
Galangal: A rhizome that looks like fresh ginger and has a similar taste. Substitute fresh ginger, or leave it out.
Tom yum paste: An aromatic seasoning used in Thai hot and sour soup.
Fish sauce: A salty liquid made from fermented fish that's used as a seasoning. It's strong-flavored and pungent, so use it sparingly.

Makes about 4 servings

4 cups (1 L) chicken or vegetable stock

2 large onions, thinly sliced

2 carrots, peeled and thinly sliced

1 shallot, thinly sliced

2 thick slices fresh ginger

2 thick slices galangal (see sidebar; optional)

1 stalk lemongrass, trimmed, gently bashed with a rolling pin and cut into quarters crosswise

1 to 2 tsp (5 to 10 mL) tom yum paste (see sidebar)

3 to 4 kaffir lime leaves (see page 140)

1 clove garlic, minced

20 large raw shrimp, peeled and deveined, or 1 lb (500 g) cubed or diced boneless, skinless chicken (optional)

1 can (14 oz/398 mL) unsweetened coconut milk, well shaken

8 oz (250 g) cremini or white button mushrooms, sliced

2 plum tomatoes, diced

2 to 3 tsp (10 to 15 mL) fish sauce (see sidebar; according to taste)

1 lb (500 g) rice noodles, soaked in cold water for 2 hours then drained (optional)

Finely chopped cilantro for garnish

1. In a large pot, combine the stock, onions, carrots, shallot, ginger, galangal (if using), lemongrass, tom yum paste, lime leaves and garlic. Bring to a boil.

2. Reduce the heat and simmer, uncovered, for 10 minutes for the flavors to develop.

3. Add the shrimp or chicken (if using). Simmer, uncovered, until the shrimp are no longer pink (about 3 minutes) or until the chicken is no longer pink inside (about 10 minutes).

4. Add the coconut milk. Bring the soup back to a simmer.

5. Add the mushrooms and tomatoes. Bring the soup back to a simmer.

6. Remove the ginger, galangal (if using) and lemongrass. Season with fish sauce to taste.

7. If using rice noodles, plunge them into a pot of boiling water to heat through, then drain well.

8. Divide the noodles among the soup bowls, then ladle the soup over the top. Garnish with a flourish of cilantro.

This recipe came from a girl called Sayon whom I met on a trip to Cambodia. Her determination to take care of her family and perseverance to succeed, despite great hardship, had a big impact on me.
—Sharon Hapton

SUMMER

W arm weather and bountiful crops of fruits and vegetables make summer a time when we enjoy some of the finest soups of the year. Hot or chilled, there's a tasty warm-weather soup here for you. From Red Pepper, Corn and Potato Chowder to Parisian Cream of Green Bean and chilly Gazpacho Andaluz, our summer soups celebrate the hard work of our local farmers.

Our Soup Sisters and Broth Brothers keep busy, too, and we have kids in summer camps make soup for their local shelters through our annual Summer Stock program.

Take advantage of summer's harvest and stock up your freezer with fresh-tasting soups to enjoy throughout the year.

Anne's Special Healing Soup

Anne Jerome, Soup Sister

There are more nutrients in this soup than most people get in a week of eating. Drink this powerful dose of vitamins, minerals, antioxidants and some protein as often as you like.

A dear friend gave me the original recipe for this soup when I was receiving chemo and radiation treatments. It can be made any time of the year, but fresh organic veggies are more available and cheaper in the summer. If you want more carbs in this soup, add carrots or sweet potatoes. If you don't mind the flatulence, add onions, broccoli or regular cabbage. And if you don't have all the ingredients on hand, use whatever you do have, because it's still healing.
—Anne Jerome

Makes about 8 servings

8 cups (2 L) vegetable stock, divided
4 to 6 stalks celery, diced
1 lb (500 g) green beans, trimmed and thinly sliced
½ head suey choy (Chinese cabbage), shredded
1 to 2 zucchini, diced
4 cups (1 L) thinly sliced kale, center ribs and stems removed (1 large bunch)
1 bunch spinach, washed
1 bunch cilantro, roots and tough stems removed, finely chopped
1 bunch Italian parsley, tough stems removed, finely chopped
2 to 3 Tbsp (30 to 45 mL) dried basil leaves

2 to 3 Tbsp (30 to 45 mL) dried oregano leaves
2 to 3 Tbsp (30 to 45 mL) ground cumin
3 cloves garlic, finely chopped
1 Tbsp (15 mL) peeled and finely chopped fresh ginger
2 to 3 sheets nori, crumbled
1 to 2 tsp (5 to 10 mL) Celtic or Himalayan salt
4 cups (1 L) chicken stock
Pepper to taste
Sour cream or plain yogurt for garnish
Finely chopped fresh dill to taste
Finely grated lemon zest to taste

1. In a large pot, bring 4 cups (1 L) of the vegetable stock to a boil, then turn off the heat.

2. Add the prepared vegetables, in the order listed, adding one type of vegetable at a time and waiting until that vegetable is almost tender-crisp before adding the next.

3. Let stand until all the vegetables are tender. If the stock cools down too much, reheat it, then remove from the heat again.

4. Add half of the remaining vegetable stock, the cilantro, parsley, basil, oregano, cumin, garlic, ginger, nori and salt. Purée the soup until almost smooth (you want to retain some of the texture).

5. Add any remaining vegetable stock and the chicken stock. Season with salt and pepper to taste.

6. Serve at room temperature or just slightly warmed to preserve the enzymes and other nutrients.

7. Ladle into bowls and add a gourmet touch of a dollop of sour cream mixed with dill and lemon zest.

Beautiful Basil-Coconut Soup with Edamame

Morey and Elizabeth Lucas, Broth Brother and Soup Sister

Makes about 4 servings

1½ cups (375 mL) shelled edamame (frozen is fine)

2½ cups (625 mL) chicken or vegetable stock

½ cup (125 mL) lightly packed fresh basil leaves, coarsely chopped

¼ tsp (1 mL) sambal oelek (see sidebar)

¾ cup (185 mL) unsweetened coconut milk

1 Tbsp (15 mL) tahini (see sidebar)

1½ tsp (7 mL) coconut sugar or brown sugar

½ tsp (2 mL) minced garlic

Salt and pepper to taste

Wakame salad (see sidebar; optional)

Additional basil leaves for garnish

1. In a small saucepan of boiling water, cook the edamame until just tender, about 4 minutes. Drain well and set aside.

2. In a medium pot, bring the stock to a simmer.

3. Add the basil and sambal oelek. Simmer, covered, for 2 minutes.

4. Add the coconut milk, tahini, coconut sugar and garlic. Simmer, covered, to blend the flavors, about 10 minutes.

5. Add the edamame to the soup. Season with salt and pepper to taste.

6. Ladle the soup into individual bowls. Add a little wakame (if using) and a fresh basil leaf to each bowl.

Sambal oelek is a spicy Indonesian condiment. Tahini is a sesame-seed paste most often used in hummus recipes. Wakame is a Japanese seaweed that's made into a slightly sweet-tasting salad. Look for the ready-made salad as well as tahini in larger grocery stores or health food stores.

To invent a soup for this book, we decided on a little innovation. We liked the idea of a soup with Asian flair but couldn't commit to any traditional combinations. Our inspiration came from fresh basil and our love of all things coconut. This creamy soup will surprise you with its simplicity.
—Morey and Elizabeth Lucas

Carrot Soup with Pesto

Nancy Arnold, Soup Sister

Makes about 4 servings

2 Tbsp (30 mL) olive oil
1½ lb (750 g) carrots, peeled, halved lengthwise and thinly sliced
1 onion, halved and thinly sliced
3 Tbsp (45 mL) all-purpose flour
5 cups (1.25 L) chicken or vegetable stock
Salt and white pepper to taste
Small basil leaves for garnish

Pesto

2 cups (500 mL) lightly packed fresh basil leaves
½ cup (125 mL) freshly grated Parmesan cheese
¼ cup (60 mL) olive oil
2 cloves garlic, coarsely chopped

1. For the soup, heat the oil in a large pot over medium heat. Add the carrots and onion. Cook, stirring often, until the onion starts to soften.

2. Add the flour. Cook, stirring often, for 4 to 5 minutes.

3. Gradually stir in the stock. Bring to a boil, stirring constantly.

4. Reduce the heat and simmer, covered, until the carrots are tender, about 15 minutes.

5. Purée the soup until smooth. Reheat gently. Season with salt and pepper to taste.

6. For the pesto, add the basil leaves, Parmesan, olive oil and garlic to a blender or food processor. Blend until finely minced and well combined.

7. Ladle the soup into bowls, add a vibrant green tablespoonful (15 mL) of the pesto to each and garnish with basil leaves.

Chickpea and Roasted Tomato Soup

Lora Kirk, Chef/Owner, Ruby Watchco, Toronto

Makes about 6 servings

1 lb (500 g) plum tomatoes
6 Tbsp (90 mL) olive oil, divided
Salt and pepper to taste
1 large onion, finely chopped
1 fennel bulb, thinly sliced
5 cloves garlic, minced
1 tsp (5 mL) Spanish sweet smoked paprika
½ tsp (2 mL) Espelette pepper (see sidebar)

4 cups (1 L) chicken or vegetable stock
2 cans (each 19 oz/540 mL) chickpeas, drained and rinsed
2 sprigs thyme
1 bay leaf
¼ cup (60 mL) freshly grated Parmesan cheese for garnish
3 Tbsp (45 mL) finely chopped parsley for garnish

1. Preheat the oven to 450°F (230°C).

2. Cut the tomatoes in half and arrange in a single layer on a large, rimmed baking sheet. Drizzle with 3 Tbsp (45 mL) of the olive oil, and season with salt and pepper to taste. Roast until the tomatoes are soft, about 30 minutes. Set aside.

3. In a large pot, heat the remaining olive oil over medium-high heat. Add the onion and fennel. Cook, stirring often, until the onion and fennel have softened.

4. Add the garlic, paprika and Espelette pepper. Cook, stirring often, for 2 minutes.

5. Stir in the roasted tomatoes, along with the stock, chickpeas, thyme and bay leaf. Bring to a boil.

6. Reduce the heat and simmer, covered, for 45 minutes.

7. Remove the thyme stems and bay leaf. Season with salt and pepper to taste.

8. Ladle into bowls and add a scattering of Parmesan and parsley.

Espelette pepper, named for the French village of Espelette, is made from chilies grown in the Basque region of France and Spain. It has a smoky-sweet flavor and subtle heat. Look for it in specialty grocery stores, or substitute Spanish hot smoked paprika.

Chilled Almond-Garlic Soup

Anna Olson, Chef, Cookbook Author and TV Host

Makes about 8 servings

3 cups (750 mL) cold water, divided
1 cup (250 mL) dry bread crumbs
2 cups (500 mL) blanched, untoasted almonds
⅓ cup (80 mL) extra virgin olive oil
3 garlic cloves, coarsely chopped
2 Tbsp (30 mL) sherry vinegar
Salt to taste
Sliced red grapes for garnish

1. In a medium bowl, combine 1½ cups (375 mL) of the water and the bread crumbs and let stand for 5 minutes.

2. Spoon the soft bread crumbs into a blender or food processor. Add the almonds, oil, garlic, vinegar and remaining water.

3. Blend until very smooth, adding more water if necessary, to achieve a smooth soup consistency.

4. Pour the soup back into the bowl and season with salt to taste. Chill for at least 2 hours before serving.

5. Just before serving, check the seasoning again (chilling can mute the soup's flavor). Ladle frosty portions into chilled bowls and scatter with sliced grapes.

Delicious dishes that I've enjoyed on holiday often inspire me to re-create the recipes at home. My husband, chef Michael Olson, and I love visiting Spain and, while tomato gazpacho is a more common chilled Spanish soup, we found this garlic-almond version simple and refreshing. Grapes are a classic garnish and add a lovely sweet-tart contrast to the richness of the soup.
—Anna Olson

Chilled Tomato Water Soup

Disnie Zivot, Soup Sister

Makes about 4 servings

Burrata is a very rich, fresh mozzarella-type cheese. Look for it in specialty cheese stores.

Made with TLC, this is a beautiful summer soup, but be sure to use the sweetest tomatoes available. Get creative with the garnishes, adding as much or as little as you wish, and choosing the freshest ingredients in season. Other additions to try are thinly sliced cucumber, peach slices, grated apple, cubed watermelon or diced jalapeños.
—Disnie Zivot

Tomato Water

6 lb (2.7 kg) ripe tomatoes, coarsely chopped

Juice of ½ lemon

1 Tbsp (15 mL) rice vinegar

1 tsp (5 mL) brown sugar, honey or your favorite sweetener

Balsamic vinegar to taste

Gremolata

½ lemon

¼ cup (60 mL) finely chopped parsley

3 to 4 fresh basil leaves, finely chopped

1 tsp (5 mL) extra virgin olive oil (optional)

Garnishes (optional)

2 to 3 yellow, orange or red grape tomatoes, cut in half

Peeled, shredded raw beet

Peeled, shredded carrot

Pitted, halved cherries or halved seedless grapes

Thinly sliced radish

Fresh pea shoots or other sprouts or micro greens

Torn burrata (see sidebar) or crumbled feta cheese

Edible flowers or small fresh basil leaves

1. For the tomato water, blend the tomatoes in a blender or food processor until they form a coarse purée.

2. Line a large colander with a double layer of cheesecloth. Set the colander over a nonreactive bowl deep enough that the base of the colander won't touch the surface of the juice that drains out of the tomatoes.

3. Tip the tomatoes into the colander. Enclose the tomatoes in the cheesecloth and tie with kitchen string.

4. Put the bowl, topped with the colander and the tomatoes, in the fridge and let drain overnight. (It's okay to wring the tomatoes in the cheesecloth at the end, if you wish. This will give you more juice but the soup won't be crystal clear.)

5. Add the lemon juice, rice vinegar, sugar and balsamic vinegar to taste to the tomato water. (Save the tomato pulp to use in other recipes, such as sauces or soups.)

6. For the gremolata, grate the zest then squeeze the juice from the lemon half. In a small bowl, stir together the lemon zest and juice, parsley, basil and oil (if using). Set aside.

7. Put your choice of garnish, except the last two, into each soup bowl. Ladle the tomato water into the bowls. Add some burrata and a sprinkling of gremolata. Finish with pretty little edible flowers (if using).

Corn Cashew Chowder with Cilantro Cream

Sarah Britton, Blogger, mynewroots.org

Makes about 4 servings

3 ears corn

1 Tbsp (15 mL) coconut oil or ghee
(see page 46)

2 tsp (10 mL) turmeric

1 tsp (5 mL) ground cumin

Cayenne to taste

2 onions, finely chopped

2 tsp (10 mL) sea salt

4 cups (1 L) vegetable stock, divided

6 cloves garlic, minced

½ cup (125 mL) raw cashews, soaked for
at least 4 hours, then drained

1 Tbsp (15 mL) fresh lime juice

Salt and pepper to taste

Extra virgin olive oil for garnish

Cracked black pepper for garnish

Cilantro Cream

1 cup (250 mL) lightly packed cilantro
leaves

½ cup (125 mL) raw cashews, soaked
for at least 4 hours, then drained and
rinsed

½ cup (125 mL) water

1 Tbsp (15 mL) fresh lime juice

1 Tbsp (15 mL) raw honey or agave

1 tsp (5 mL) sea salt

½ small clove garlic (optional)

Pinch of cayenne (optional)

1. For the soup, cut the kernels from the ears of corn (see page 26). Set kernels aside.

2. In a large pot, heat the oil over medium heat. Add the turmeric, cumin and cayenne. Cook, stirring, until fragrant, about 1 minute.

3. Add the onions and salt. Cook, stirring often, until the onions have softened. If the bottom of the pot becomes dry, add a little of the vegetable stock. Add the garlic and cook, stirring, for 30 seconds.

4. Add the corn to the pot and stir to coat with the spices. Cook, stirring often, for 5 minutes. Add the remaining stock and bring to a boil.

5. Reduce the heat and simmer until the corn is bright yellow and sweet, about 5 minutes.

6. Meanwhile, for the cilantro cream, put all the ingredients in a blender (not a food processor) and blend on high speed until smooth. Season to taste with more salt or cayenne (if using). (Leftovers can be stored in a sealed glass container in the fridge for up to 3 days.)

7. Once the corn is cooked, remove the pot from the heat. Scoop out a few tablespoonfuls of the corn kernels to use as garnish.

8. Transfer the soup to a blender, add the cashews to the soup and purée until smooth.

9. Return to the pot and stir in the lime juice. Reheat gently. If the soup seems too thick, add a little water. Season with salt and pepper to taste.

10. Ladle into bowls and top each portion prettily with a little cilantro cream, a drizzle of olive oil, a few of the reserved corn kernels and plenty of cracked black pepper.

Corn Bisque

Mark McEwan, Celebrity Chef, Restaurant Owner and Cookbook Author

Makes about 4 servings

2 sweet red peppers, divided	4 cloves garlic, minced
2 sweet green peppers, divided	1 cup (250 mL) white wine
1 large sweet potato, peeled and divided	4 cups (1 L) chicken or vegetable stock
8 ears corn in their husks, divided	Salt and pepper to taste
¼ cup (60 mL) olive oil, divided	1 tsp (5 mL) truffle oil for garnish
1 Spanish onion, finely chopped	(optional)

This sweet purée delivers one of the most memorable and evocative flavors of the Canadian summer in an elegant form without the hassle of dribbling butter down your chin.
—Mark McEwan

1. Preheat the barbecue to medium.

2. Chop 1 red and 1 green pepper, discarding the seeds. Dice the remaining peppers, discarding the seeds. Chop three-quarters of the sweet potato and dice the remainder. Set aside.

3. Grill the whole ears of corn in their husks, turning often, until the kernels are just cooked, 10 to 12 minutes.

4. When cool enough to handle, shuck the corn. Cut the kernels from the ears of corn (see page 26). Set kernels aside. Cut the ears crosswise into 6 or 7 pieces each.

5. In a large pot, heat 2 Tbsp (30 mL) of the oil over medium heat. Add the onion, garlic and chopped-up ears. Cook, stirring often, for 2 minutes. Add the chopped peppers, chopped sweet potato and three-quarters of the corn kernels. Cook, stirring often, until the onion is softened.

6. Add the wine and bring to a boil, stirring to scrape up any browned bits from the bottom of the pot. Add the stock and salt and pepper to taste, and bring to a simmer. Cook, uncovered, until the vegetables are tender, about 30 minutes.

7. Remove the chopped-up ears. Purée the soup until smooth. Reheat gently.

8. Meanwhile, have ready a bowl of ice water. In a medium saucepan of boiling water, blanch the diced red and green peppers for 45 to 60 seconds. With a slotted spoon, remove the peppers to the ice water. Repeat the process with the diced sweet potato. Drain well.

9. When ready to serve, heat the remaining oil in a small skillet over medium heat. Add the blanched peppers, sweet potato and remaining corn. Cook, stirring often, until the vegetables are heated through and starting to soften.

10. Ladle the hot bisque into bowls and pile a generous spoonful of the sautéed vegetables in the center. For a luxe touch, finish with a drizzle of truffle oil (if using).

Gazpacho Andaluz

Daniel Hayes, The London Chef, Victoria

Makes about 6 servings

6 cups (1.5 L) cold water
8 ripe tomatoes, cored and cut into large chunks
1 sweet red pepper, seeded and cut into large chunks
½ Spanish or red onion, cut into large chunks
½ English cucumber, cut into large chunks
¼ stale baguette, ripped into pieces
¼ cup (60 mL) sherry vinegar
¼ cup (60 mL) olive oil
2 Tbsp (30 mL) tomato paste
1 clove garlic, coarsely chopped
1 tsp (5 mL) granulated sugar
Salt and pepper to taste

1. In a large nonreactive bowl, combine all the ingredients.
2. In a food processor or blender, blend the ingredients in batches until smooth.
3. Pour the soup back into the bowl and season with more vinegar, sugar, salt and pepper to taste.
4. Chill well and serve ice-cold in chilled glasses or bowls.

Gazpacho is the perfect summer dish. Who says you need fire to cook? Have fun with this recipe. Play around with the salt, sugar and vinegar to create the perfect balance of salty, sweet and tart.
—Dan Hayes

Golden Chanterelle Chowder with Double-Smoked Bacon and Corn

Anthony Walsh, Corporate Executive Chef, Oliver & Bonacini Restaurants, Toronto

Makes about 4 servings

Made with homemade stock, this is a gluten-free soup but, if you're using purchased chicken stock, check the ingredients carefully as some brands may contain gluten.

When I worked for chef Jamie Kennedy, I was always amazed by a dish he made called chanterelles à la crème. *The flavor, harmony and texture of that dish and the technique involved in its preparation directly influenced this recipe. Later I added the fresh corn to complement the soup's chanterelles and double-smoked bacon.*
—Anthony Walsh

2 ears corn
3 Tbsp (45 mL) olive oil
³⁄₄ cup (185 mL) finely chopped double-smoked bacon
2 bay leaves
1 sprig thyme
1 cup (250 mL) minced shallots
¹⁄₂ cup (125 mL) finely chopped celery
2 cloves garlic, minced
2 cups (500 mL) chanterelle mushrooms, cleaned and coarsely chopped

³⁄₄ cup (185 mL) white wine
3 cups (750 mL) chicken stock
2 cups (500 mL) whipping cream (35% MF)
1 cup (250 mL) crème fraîche (see page 182)
1 Tbsp (15 mL) unsalted butter
Salt and pepper to taste
Finely chopped chives for garnish

1. Cut the kernels from the ears of corn (see page 26). Set kernels aside. Cut ears in half crosswise.

2. In a large pot, heat the oil over medium-high heat. Add the bacon, bay leaves and thyme. Cook, stirring often, until the bacon fat renders.

3. Add the shallots, celery, garlic and empty corn ears. Cook, stirring often, until the celery has softened. Stir in the chanterelles.

4. Add the wine and bring to a boil. Boil until the wine has reduced by about two-thirds. (Have a glass yourself while you're waiting!)

5. Add the stock and bring to a boil. Boil until the liquid has reduced by one-third.

6. Add the whipping cream and bring to a boil. Reduce the heat and simmer, uncovered, for about 20 minutes.

7. Remove the bay leaves, thyme stem and corn ears. Add the crème fraîche and reserved corn kernels. Simmer for about 2 minutes.

8. Remove the pot from the heat. Lightly pulse the soup with an immersion blender to give it a rustic, porridge-like texture. Reheat gently.

9. Remove the pot from the heat and stir in the butter until it melts. Season with salt and pepper to taste. Ladle into bowls and garnish with a dusting of chives.

Home-Style Chicken-Veggie Soup with Basil

Kimi Nakamura, Soup Sister and Owner, Nanatari, Calgary

Makes about 6 servings

1 Tbsp (15 mL) olive oil or butter
1 boneless, skinless chicken breast, cut into bite-size pieces
Sea salt and pepper to taste
½ onion, chopped
2 carrots, peeled and diced
2 stalks celery, diced
2 plum tomatoes, chopped
4 cups (1 L) chicken or vegetable stock
1 large bunch fresh basil, coarsely chopped
Corn tortilla chips for garnish or serving

1. In a large pot, heat the oil over medium-high heat. Lightly season the chicken with salt and pepper to taste.

2. Add the chicken to the pot. Cook, stirring often, until lightly browned.

3. Add the onion to the pot. Cook, stirring often, until the onion starts to soften.

4. Reduce the heat to medium. Add the carrots and celery. Cook, stirring often, for 2 to 3 minutes.

5. Add the tomatoes. Cook, stirring often, until the tomatoes start to soften.

6. Add the stock. Bring to a boil.

7. Reduce the heat and simmer, uncovered, until the vegetables are tender, about 10 minutes.

8. Remove the pot from the heat. Stir in the basil, and season with salt and pepper to taste.

9. Ladle into bowls. Add a crunchy scattering of tortilla chips or serve the chips on the side.

My passion is playing in the kitchen and creating recipes. A bunch of fresh basil was the inspiration for this chicken soup, which illustrates the guiding principle behind the cooking seminars I conduct: food prepared with love and gratitude nourishes our souls as well as our bodies. For the garnish, choose tortilla chips made from non–genetically modified corn, like Que Pasa chips.
—Kimi Nakamura

Navy Bean and Pasta Soup with Pistou

Christine Cushing, TV Chef and Cookbook Author

Makes about 6 servings

2 Tbsp (30 mL) olive oil

2 leeks (white parts only), thinly sliced

1 large onion, finely chopped

2 carrots, peeled, halved lengthwise and
thinly sliced

2 stalks celery, thinly sliced

3 small cloves garlic, thinly sliced

3 sprigs fresh thyme

2 bay leaves

8 cups (2 L) chicken or vegetable stock

1 can (19 oz/540 mL) navy or cannellini
beans, drained and rinsed

¾ cup (185 mL) good-quality small shell
pasta

Salt and pepper to taste

Freshly grated Parmesan cheese for
garnish (optional)

Pistou

1 large bunch basil, washed and dried,
leaves picked off

⅓ cup (80 mL) extra virgin olive oil

1 small clove garlic, crushed

1. For the soup, heat the oil in a large pot over high heat. Add the leeks and onion.
   Cook, stirring often, until the onion has softened.

2. Add the carrots, celery, garlic, thyme and bay leaves. Cook, stirring often,
   until golden.

3. Add the stock and bring to a boil.

4. Reduce the heat and simmer, covered, until the vegetables are tender, about
   15 minutes.

5. Add the beans, pasta and salt and pepper to taste. Bring to a gentle simmer. Cook,
   covered, until the pasta is tender, 7 to 9 minutes. Remove the thyme stems and
   bay leaves.

6. Meanwhile, for the pistou, combine all the ingredients in a food processor or mini
   chopper. Pulse until smooth.

7. Ladle up bowlfuls of the soup and add a heaping dollop of pistou to each bowl, then
   sprinkle with Parmesan (if using).

*This soup is a
Mediterranean favorite
of mine which you
can adapt by using
almost any variety of
vegetables you have on
hand. The basil and
garlic pistou added at
the end gives the soup
a bold kick.*
—Christine Cushing

Out of tomato season, replace the fresh plum tomatoes with one drained can (28 oz/796 mL).

If you don't have a food mill, process the tomato mixture, in batches, in a food processor, then strain through a fine-mesh sieve, discarding the solids in the sieve.

I first tasted this soup in Italy, at a restaurant called Cibreo in Florence. The way the waiter's eyes lit up while describing a soup called Pappa al Pomodoro had me hooked. Thickened with bread, at Cibreo this tomato soup was served with a fork! When we got back to the villa we were renting, we convinced its owner, the charming Liria Costantino, to teach us how to make the soup. This is her version of Pappa al Pomodoro.
—Cindy Feingold

Pappa al Pomodoro (Italian Tomato-Bread Soup)

Cindy Feingold, Soup Sister

Makes about 4 servings

2 lb (1 kg) plum tomatoes (about 8 to 10), cut into quarters

4 large green onions, cut in half crosswise

20 fresh basil leaves, divided

1 tsp (5 mL) salt

Pinch of red chili flakes (optional)

¼ cup (60 mL) olive oil

3 cloves garlic, lightly crushed

4 whole cloves

½ loaf stale Italian bread (at least 3 days old), cut into 1-inch (2.5 cm) chunks

Extra virgin olive oil for garnish

Additional thinly sliced fresh basil leaves for garnish

1. In a large nonreactive pot, combine the tomatoes, green onions, 10 of the basil leaves, the salt and chili flakes (if using). Bring to a simmer over medium heat. Cook, uncovered, for 20 minutes. Remove the green onions.

2. In two batches, pass the tomato mixture through a food mill (see sidebar) into a large, nonreactive bowl. Discard the seeds and skin.

3. In the same pot, heat the oil over medium-low heat. Add the garlic, whole cloves and remaining basil leaves. Cook, stirring often, until the mixture smells incredibly fragrant (do not let the garlic brown; this is most important).

4. Add the reserved tomato pulp to the pot. Bring to a simmer. Cook, uncovered, for 10 minutes.

5. In a food processor, process the bread chunks in batches to make bread crumbs.

6. Remove the garlic and whole cloves from the tomato mixture. Stir in half of the bread crumbs. Look at the consistency of the soup: it should be quite thick, like porridge. Add the remaining bread crumbs, if desired. (I used the entire amount.)

7. Simmer for 2 or 3 minutes. (The soup can be made several hours ahead and will keep at room temperature. Reheat before serving.)

8. Ladle into bowls. Drizzle each portion with some fruity extra virgin olive oil and a drift of thinly sliced basil.

Parisian Cream of Green Bean with White Wine and Herbs

Tara McIntosh, Soup Sister

Makes about 6 servings

2 lb (1 kg) green beans, trimmed	2 cups (500 mL) whipping cream
2 Tbsp (30 mL) olive oil	(35% MF) or low-fat evaporated milk
1 onion, finely chopped	1 cup (250 mL) white wine
½ cup (125 mL) diced celery	3 Tbsp (45 mL) finely chopped chives
½ cup (125 mL) peeled and diced carrot	3 Tbsp (45 mL) finely chopped fresh dill
4 cloves garlic, minced	3 Tbsp (45 mL) finely chopped parsley
¼ cup (60 mL) butter	3 Tbsp (45 mL) fresh thyme leaves
⅓ cup (80 mL) all-purpose flour	Salt and pepper to taste
8 cups (2 L) chicken stock	Fresh parsley for garnish

1. Have ready a bowl of ice water. In a large saucepan of boiling, salted water, cook the beans until tender, about 15 minutes. Drain well. Immediately put the beans in the ice water. Set aside.

2. In a large pot, heat the oil over medium heat. Add the onion, celery, carrot and garlic. Cook, stirring often, until the onion has softened (make sure the garlic doesn't brown). Scrape the onion mixture out of the pot and set aside. Wipe out the pot.

3. In the same pot, heat the butter over medium heat. Add the flour. Cook, stirring, for about 15 seconds.

4. Gradually whisk in the stock and cream, whisking constantly to avoid lumps.

5. Add the wine, drained beans and reserved onion mixture. Bring to a boil, stirring constantly.

6. Add the chives, dill, parsley and thyme.

7. Reduce the heat and simmer, covered, until the vegetables are tender, 10 or 15 minutes.

8. Purée the soup until smooth. Reheat gently. Season with salt and pepper to taste.

9. Ladle up vibrant bowlfuls, garnish with parsley and celebrate green bean season.

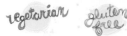

Peaches and Cream Soup

Pierre A. Lamielle, Chef and Cookbook Author

Makes about 6 servings

Ginger ice cubes are a great garnish for this soup—they chill it down and add a hit of flavor. Simply pour ginger ale into an ice cube tray, then freeze until solid.

6 very ripe peaches
2 cups (500 mL) milk (approx.)
1-inch (2.5 cm) piece fresh ginger, peeled and grated
1 tsp (5 mL) ground ginger
Pinch of salt
1 cup (250 mL) whipping cream (35% MF)
Honey to taste
Ginger ice cubes (see sidebar)

Be cool, Daddy-o. This is an awesome summer soup that capitalizes on the natural sweetness of fresh, juicy peaches. Even though this soup is served ice cold, the ginger will warm your palate with a little heat. The soup also makes a great dessert to sip on after a heavy-duty barbecue (add a little peach schnapps to each serving to tickle the taste buds).
—Pierre A. Lamielle

1. Bring a large pot of water to a boil. Have ready a large bowl of ice water.

2. Place the peaches in the boiling water for 1 minute. With a slotted spoon, remove the peaches and immediately place in the ice water.

3. Drain the peaches. Remove the peel. Chop the peaches, discarding the pits. Set aside.

4. In a large saucepan, combine 2 cups (500 mL) milk, fresh ginger, ground ginger and salt. Bring to a boil.

5. Add the peaches. Reduce the heat and simmer until the peaches soften slightly, about 2 minutes.

6. Purée the soup until smooth. Strain through a fine-mesh sieve into a large bowl.

7. Stir in the cream. If the soup is too thick, stir in a little more milk. Add honey to taste if necessary. Chill for at least 2 hours.

8. Ladle up ice-cold bowlfuls, add a couple of ginger ice cubes to each portion, and chill out.

Perfect Lobster Bisque

Paul Rogalski, Culinary Director/Co-owner, Rouge Restaurant and Bistro
Rouge, Calgary

Makes about 4 servings

2 live lobsters (each 1½ lb/750 g)
½ cup (125 mL) butter
4 stalks celery, diced
2 carrots, peeled and diced
1 large onion, finely chopped
2 cloves garlic, minced
1 cup (250 mL) tomato paste
2 Tbsp (30 mL) finely chopped fresh thyme
2 Tbsp (30 mL) dried tarragon leaves
15 whole black peppercorns

½ cinnamon stick
6 cups (1.5 L) fish stock
½ cup (125 mL) white wine
⅓ cup (80 mL) Cognac
½ cup (125 mL) arborio rice
1 cup (250 mL) whipping cream (35% MF)
Tabasco sauce and Worcestershire sauce to taste
Salt to taste
White summer truffle, shaved (optional)

1. Preheat the oven to 300°F (150°C).

2. Cook and shell the lobsters as described on page 35, reserving the shells. Dice the lobster meat and refrigerate until ready to serve.

3. Put the lobster shells in a shallow roasting pan and bake until they're bright red and dry, about 20 minutes. Let cool, then smash the shells into smaller pieces.

4. In a large pot, melt the butter over medium heat. Add the lobster shells, celery, carrots, onion and garlic. Cook, stirring often, until the onion starts to soften.

5. Stir in the tomato paste, thyme, tarragon, peppercorns and cinnamon stick.

6. Stir in the stock, then the wine and Cognac. Bring to a boil.

7. Reduce the heat and simmer, uncovered, until the vegetables are tender, about 30 minutes.

8. Strain through a fine-mesh sieve into a clean pot and bring to a simmer.

9. Add the rice and simmer, uncovered, until tender, about 20 minutes.

10. Purée the soup until smooth. Return to the pot and stir in the cream.

11. Reheat gently and season with Tabasco sauce, Worcestershire sauce and salt to taste.

12. Strain once more through a fine-mesh sieve, then add the reserved lobster meat to the soup.

13. Ladle into bowls and garnish with luxurious shavings of fresh truffle (if using).

Quinoa Soup with Peas and Fresh Mint

Kalayra Angelyys, Soup Sister and Owner of Snacker Cracker

Makes about 6 servings

2 Tbsp (30 mL) butter, divided
1 Tbsp (15 mL) olive oil
3 oz (90 g) thickly sliced bacon, diced
2 green onions, finely chopped
1 cup (250 mL) quinoa, rinsed and drained
6 cups (1.5 L) chicken or vegetable stock
2 cups (500 mL) peas (fresh or frozen)
1½ cups (375 mL) firmly packed fresh mint leaves, finely chopped
Pepper to taste
Freshly grated Parmesan cheese for garnish

1. In a large pot, heat 1 Tbsp (15 mL) of the butter and the oil over medium heat. Add the bacon. Cook, stirring often, until the bacon is crisp.

2. Add the green onions. Cook, stirring often, until the onions have softened but are not brown.

3. Add the quinoa. Cook, stirring often, to toast it a little.

4. Add the stock. Bring to a boil.

5. Reduce the heat and simmer, covered, until the quinoa is tender, about 15 minutes.

6. Add the peas. Simmer, uncovered, until the peas are tender, about 5 minutes.

7. Stir in the mint, the remaining butter and pepper to taste.

8. Ladle into bowls and shower each portion with some Parmesan.

For a vegetarian option, use vegetable stock and omit the bacon.

I have so much fresh mint growing in my garden that I love to use it up in different dishes. Here it gives this soup a fresh, summery feel. Plus, I like the way quinoa (a seed, not a grain) adds an extra boost of protein to the soup. If you have any soup left over the next day, you may need to add some extra stock or water, for the quinoa will absorb liquid as it stands.
—Kalayra Angelyys

Quinoa is a healthy seed that contains essential amino acids, such as lysine. It's a complete protein and a source of calcium and phosphorous. A natural, but bitter-tasting, coating called saponin is removed from the seeds after harvesting, but it's always a good idea to rinse the quinoa a couple of times before cooking. Replacing the cream with coconut milk makes this refreshing soup vegan-friendly.

The origins of vichyssoise are subject to debate, but it seems to have found its roots in the childhood of a French chef called Louis Diat. Working in New York City around 1924, Diat created a refreshing sensation by chilling the potato and leek soup of his homeland.
—Thierry Meret

Quinoa Vichyssoise with Grilled Apple and Mint

Thierry Meret, Executive Director and Chef de Cuisine, Cuisine et Château Interactive Culinary Centre, Calgary

Makes about 4 servings

¼ cup (60 mL) quinoa, rinsed and drained

3 Tbsp (45 mL) olive oil, divided

1 cup (250 mL) chopped leek (white part only)

1 tsp (5 mL) finely grated lemon zest

1 tsp (5 mL) sea salt

1 tsp (5 mL) white pepper

½ tsp (2 mL) ground coriander

4 cups (1 L) vegetable stock

1 cup (250 mL) chopped leek (pale-green part only)

½ cup (125 mL) lightly packed mint leaves

1 Granny Smith apple, cored and sliced

½ cup (125 mL) half-and-half cream (10% MF; optional)

Additional mint leaves for garnish

1. Put the quinoa in a saucepan and add enough water to cover it generously. Bring to a boil. Reduce the heat and simmer until the quinoa is soft but not mushy, about 15 minutes.

2. Drain through a fine-mesh sieve. Rinse under cold water, drain again and set aside.

3. In a large pot, heat 2 Tbsp (30 mL) of the oil over medium heat. Add the white leek, lemon zest, salt, pepper and coriander. Cook, stirring often, until soft but not brown.

4. Add the stock. Bring to a boil.

5. Reduce the heat and simmer, covered, for about 10 minutes.

6. Add the green leek and simmer for 5 minutes.

7. Add the mint and half of the reserved cooked quinoa.

8. Purée the soup until smooth. (Strain through a fine-mesh sieve if you wish.)

9. Pour the soup into a large bowl and stir in the remaining quinoa. Chill for at least 2 hours before serving.

10. Meanwhile, preheat the barbecue to medium.

11. Brush the apple slices with the remaining oil. Grill until tender and well-marked with grill marks, 2 to 3 minutes on each side.

12. Stir the cream (if using) into the chilled soup. Ladle into chilled bowls and garnish with mint leaves and the grilled apple slices.

Rainy Day Roasted Tomato Soup

Heather Reisman, CEO, Indigo Books & Music Inc.

Makes about 6 servings

6 to 8 ripe tomatoes, coarsely chopped
2 red onions, coarsely chopped
3 Tbsp (45 mL) olive oil
2 cloves garlic, coarsely chopped
1 Tbsp (15 mL) dried oregano leaves
Salt and pepper to taste
1 can (28 oz/796 mL) crushed tomatoes
2 cups (500 mL) chicken or vegetable stock
6 large fresh basil leaves, divided
Extra virgin olive oil for drizzling (optional)

Roast tomatoes add wonderful depth of flavor to this soup. If you don't have access to an outdoor grill—or the weather isn't cooperating—this recipe, which uses your broiler and oven, replicates that smoky, outdoor taste.

—Heather Reisman

1. Preheat the broiler to high.

2. In a large bowl, toss together the fresh tomatoes, onions, olive oil, garlic, oregano, and salt and pepper to taste.

3. Spread out the tomato mixture on a large, rimmed baking sheet. Broil about 4 inches (10 cm) from the element, rotating the baking sheet once or twice, until the mixture starts to char, 5 to 7 minutes. Keep an eye on the tomatoes so they don't burn completely—a few black spots are okay.

4. Turn the broiler off and the oven on to 350°F (180°C). Roast the tomato mixture for 30 minutes.

5. In a large pot, combine the canned tomatoes, stock and 5 of the basil leaves. Bring to a boil.

6. Add the roast tomato mixture. Reduce the heat and simmer, covered, for 15 minutes.

7. Purée the soup until smooth. Reheat gently.

8. Coarsely chop the remaining basil leaf. Ladle the soup into bowls. Scatter with the basil and drizzle with extra virgin olive oil (if using).

Red Pepper, Corn and Potato Chowder

Ken Canavan, Chef, Cilantro Restaurant, Calgary

Makes about 8 servings

2 Tbsp (30 mL) vegetable oil

7 sweet red peppers, seeded and coarsely chopped

3 russet potatoes, peeled and coarsely chopped

2 onions, coarsely chopped

8 cups (2 L) chicken or vegetable stock

4 cups (1 L) water

1 Tbsp (15 mL) dried thyme leaves

2 tsp (10 mL) salt

2 tsp (10 mL) pepper

1 tsp (5 mL) Cajun blackening spice (see sidebar)

2 cups (500 mL) whipping cream (35% MF)

3 oz (90 g) cream cheese

4 cups (1 L) corn kernels (fresh or frozen)

3 Tbsp (45 mL) finely chopped parsley for garnish

Cajun blackening spice is a lusty combo of paprika, garlic, cayenne and other herbs and spices specially designed for seasoning blackened chicken or fish. Buy it online from The Silk Road (silkroadspices.ca).

1. In a large pot, heat the oil over medium heat. Add the peppers, potatoes and onions. Cook, stirring often, until the onions have softened and are golden.

2. Add the stock, water, thyme, salt, pepper and blackening spice. Bring to a boil.

3. Reduce the heat and simmer, covered, until the potatoes are tender, about 25 minutes.

4. Remove the pot from the heat and stir in the cream and cream cheese until the cream cheese has melted.

5. Purée the soup until smooth. Add the corn. Bring back to a simmer and simmer until the corn is tender.

6. Ladle out hearty bowlfuls and scatter generously with parsley.

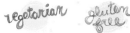

Roasted Red Pepper Soup with Goat Cheese and Basil Pesto

Carrie Rau, Head Chef, Dish Cooking Studio, Toronto

Makes about 8 servings

1 Tbsp (15 mL) canola oil
1 onion, finely chopped
2 cloves garlic, minced
2 large bushy sprigs fresh thyme, leaves picked off and finely chopped
¼ cup (60 mL) white wine
4 cups (1 L) vegetable stock
4 to 5 sweet red peppers, roasted, peeled, seeded and chopped (see sidebar)
1 cup (250 mL) canned whole tomatoes with their juice, coarsely chopped
Salt and pepper to taste
1 Yukon Gold potato, peeled and cut into 1-inch (2.5 cm) pieces
1 cup (250 mL) crumbled soft goat cheese
Red wine vinegar to taste
Honey to taste
Basil Pesto (see page 180)

Roasted Sweet Peppers
Preheat the broiler to high. Cut the peppers in half lengthwise. Arrange, cut sides down, on a large rimmed baking sheet. Broil about 4 inches (10 cm) from the element until the peppers are charred, 10 to 15 minutes. Transfer to a large bowl and let stand until cool.

1. In a large pot, heat the oil over medium heat. Add the onion, garlic and thyme. Cook, stirring often, until the onion has softened.

2. Add the wine. Bring to a boil. Simmer, uncovered, for 2 minutes, stirring to scrape up any browned bits from the bottom of the pot.

3. Add the stock, roasted peppers and tomatoes. Season with salt and pepper to taste. Bring to a boil.

4. Reduce the heat. Add the potatoes. Simmer, uncovered, until the potatoes are tender, 25 to 30 minutes.

5. Add the goat cheese, stirring until it melts. Purée the soup until smooth.

6. Reheat gently. Season with vinegar, honey, and salt and pepper to taste.

7. Ladle into bowls and top with a dollop of basil pesto.

cont'd on page 180

Basil Pesto

1 bunch fresh basil, leaves only
2 Tbsp (30 mL) freshly grated Parmesan cheese
1 clove garlic, minced
½ to ¾ cup (125 to 185 mL) olive oil
Juice of ½ lemon
Salt and pepper to taste

1. In a food processor, combine the basil, Parmesan and garlic. Pulse until finely minced.

2. With the motor running, gradually add ½ cup (125 mL) of the oil through the feed tube. Process until well combined, adding more oil if the pesto is too thick.

3. Scrape the pesto into a bowl. Stir in the lemon juice and salt and pepper to taste.

Roasted Tomato–Gin Soup

Rob Feenie, Food Concept Architect, Cactus Restaurants Ltd., Vancouver

Makes about 8 servings

4 lb (2 kg) plum tomatoes, cut in half
⅓ cup (80 mL) finely chopped fresh thyme, divided
2 Tbsp (30 mL) finely chopped fresh oregano
2 tsp (10 mL) salt
1 tsp (5 mL) pepper
4 cups (1 L) vegetable or chicken stock

1 Tbsp (15 mL) butter
1 cup (250 mL) gin
1 cup (250 mL) lightly packed fresh basil leaves
Crème fraîche (see page 182)
2 Tbsp (30 mL) extra virgin olive oil
8 Parmesan tuiles (see page 182)

1. Preheat the oven to 250°F (120°C).

2. In a large bowl, toss the plum tomatoes with 2 Tbsp (30 mL) of the thyme, the oregano, and salt and pepper.

3. Arrange the tomatoes, cut sides up, on a large, rimmed baking sheet lined with parchment paper. Roast until the tomatoes have shrunk and look wrinkly and most of their moisture has evaporated, about 3 hours.

4. Transfer the tomatoes to a large pot. Add the stock and remaining thyme. Bring to a boil.

5. Reduce the heat and simmer, uncovered, for about 1 hour.

6. In a small saucepan, melt the butter over medium heat. Add the gin and heat briefly. Standing back, ignite the gin and allow it to flame. When the flame dies down, add the gin mixture to the soup, along with the basil.

7. Purée the soup until smooth. Reheat gently. Season with salt and pepper to taste.

8. Ladle into bowls and top each with a dollop of crème fraîche and a drizzle of extra virgin olive oil. Serve with the Parmesan tuiles.

cont'd on page 182

Crème Fraîche
Makes about 2 cups (500 mL)

1 cup (250 mL) buttermilk
1 cup (250 mL) whipping cream (35% MF)

1. In a medium saucepan, combine the buttermilk and whipping cream. Bring almost to a boil over medium-high heat.
2. Immediately remove the saucepan from the heat, cover, and let stand at room temperature until thickened, about 24 hours. (The crème fraîche will keep for up to 5 days in the fridge.)

Parmesan Tuiles
Makes 8

2 cups (500 mL) finely grated Parmesan cheese

1. Preheat the oven to 350°F (180°C).
2. Spread the Parmesan evenly into a round on a large baking sheet lined with parchment paper.
3. Bake until melted and golden brown, about 5 minutes.
4. Remove from the oven and let cool completely on the baking sheet.
5. Snap the Parmesan round into 8 even-size pieces.

Soba Noodle Soup with Seared Beef and Enoki Mushrooms

Rose Reisman, Cookbook Author and Health & Wellness Entrepreneur

Makes about 6 servings

Nonstick vegetable oil spray

6 oz (175 g) strip loin steak, fat trimmed

2 tsp (10 mL) peeled and minced fresh ginger

2 tsp (10 mL) minced fresh garlic

8 cups (2 L) chicken or beef stock

2 Tbsp (30 mL) low-sodium soy sauce

3 oz (90 g) soba noodles

1 cup (250 mL) sliced bok choy

1 cup (250 mL) enoki mushrooms

½ cup (125 mL) trimmed, sliced snow peas

2 large green onions, chopped

2 tsp (10 mL) sesame oil

½ cup (125 mL) bean sprouts for garnish

3 Tbsp (45 mL) finely chopped cilantro or parsley for garnish

1. Spray a grill pan with vegetable oil and heat over medium-high heat. Sear the steak just until rare in the middle, about 2 minutes on each side.

2. Remove the steak to a cutting board, cover loosely with foil, and let rest for a few minutes. Slice very thinly against the grain and set aside.

3. Spray a large pot with vegetable oil and heat over medium heat. Add the ginger and garlic. Cook, stirring, until fragrant, about 2 minutes.

4. Add the stock and soy sauce. Bring to a boil. Add the noodles and return to a boil.

5. Reduce the heat and simmer, uncovered, until the noodles are tender, about 4 minutes.

6. Add the bok choy, mushrooms and snow peas. Simmer until tender-crisp, about 2 minutes.

7. Add the reserved sliced beef, green onions and sesame oil. Ladle into soup bowls and garnish each serving with a flourish of bean sprouts and cilantro.

If you prefer, substitute sliced chicken, pork or tofu for the beef, searing them as described in the recipe. If using chicken or pork, be sure to cook them thoroughly in the broth until no longer pink inside before serving.

For a vegetarian and gluten-free version of this recipe, use tofu instead of beef and rice noodles instead of soba.

This simplified version of Vietnamese pho is simple to make and is a complete meal in one bowl. Enoki mushrooms are small and creamy white mushrooms with tall stalks. One cup (250 mL) provides 2 grams of protein and 2 grams of fiber, with only 24 calories and 0 grams of fat. If you can't find enoki, use button mushrooms, although cook these before adding to the soup.
—Rose Reisman

So-Easy Mushroom Soup

Elizabeth Baird, Food Writer and Cookbook Author

Makes about 4 servings

2 Tbsp (30 mL) butter
4 cups (1 L) thinly sliced mushrooms
1 onion, finely chopped
1 large clove garlic, minced
¼ cup (60 mL) all-purpose flour
4 cups (1 L) chicken or vegetable stock
2 sprigs fresh thyme (or 1 tsp/5 mL dried thyme leaves, crumbled)
1 bay leaf
¼ tsp (1 mL) pepper
¾ cup (185 mL) light cream (5% MF) or whole milk
Salt to taste
2 Tbsp (30 mL) finely chopped parsley for garnish
2 Tbsp (30 mL) finely chopped chives for garnish

Forget the "cream-of" canned mushroom soup; this homemade version is so much tastier. It's hearty enough for a soup-and-sandwich lunch, yet sufficiently fancy to impress guests. If you prefer, omit the cream and serve the soup as is with a nice dollop of yogurt or sour cream on top. Try using canola or olive oil instead of butter, or sliced cremini mushrooms or shiitake mushroom caps instead of cultivated white mushrooms.
—Elizabeth Baird

1. In a large, heavy-bottomed pot, melt the butter over medium heat. Add the mushrooms, onion and garlic.

2. Increase the heat to medium-high and cook, stirring often, until the moisture has evaporated and the mushrooms are starting to become golden around the edges, about 5 minutes. Listen for the sizzle.

3. Reduce the heat to medium. Stir in the flour, coating the mushroom mixture with it. Cook, stirring, until the flour on the bottom of the pot starts to brown.

4. Add the stock, stirring constantly. Add the thyme, bay leaf and pepper. Bring back to a simmer.

5. Reduce the heat and simmer, covered, until the soup has a good mushroom flavor and has thickened, about 15 minutes.

6. Stir in the cream and heat until steaming. Remove the thyme stems (if using) and bay leaf. Season with salt and pepper to taste.

7. Ladle up classy bowlfuls and top each with a sprinkle of parsley and chives.

Spot Prawn Bisque with Coriander-Dusted Potato Beignets

Matthew Batey, Executive Chef, Mission Hill Family Estate Winery, Kelowna, B.C.

Makes about 4 servings

⅓ cup (80 mL) butter

2 cups (500 mL) spot prawn shells, cleaned and chopped

2 onions, finely chopped

2 leeks (white parts only), thinly sliced

2 stalks celery, finely diced

2 carrots, peeled and finely diced

6 sprigs thyme

¼ cup (60 mL) Cognac

2 Tbsp (30 mL) tomato paste

⅓ cup (80 mL) all-purpose flour

4 cups (1 L) chicken stock

⅓ cup (80 mL) whipping cream (35% MF)

Coriander-dusted potato beignets (see page 187) for serving

¼ cup (60 mL) whipping cream (35% MF)

Finely chopped cilantro for garnish

Spot prawn season runs from May through June. Outside B.C. you can find frozen spot prawns at better fish stores.

1. For the bisque, melt the butter in a large pot over medium heat. Add the prawn shells and cook, stirring often, until the shells are bright red.

2. Add the onions, leeks, celery, carrots and thyme. Cook, stirring often, until the onions have softened.

3. Add the Cognac and, standing back, ignite the Cognac and allow it to flame. When the flame dies down, add the tomato paste and cook for 1 minute, stirring to prevent it from burning.

4. Add the flour and cook for 1 minute, stirring to coat all the ingredients with the flour.

5. Add the stock and bring to a simmer, stirring constantly. Simmer, uncovered and stirring occasionally, until the vegetables are tender, about 10 minutes. Stir in the cream.

6. Strain the bisque through a fine-mesh sieve, reserving the shells and vegetables but discarding the thyme. Return the liquid to the pot.

7. In a blender (not a food processor), blend the shells and vegetables in batches, along with some liquid from the pot, until smooth. Strain this blended liquid through a fine-mesh sieve and add to the bisque in the pot. Reheat gently.

8. Just before serving, prepare the potato beignets (see page 187).

9. Whip the cream until it holds soft peaks. Fold the cilantro into the cream to taste.

10. Ladle the soup into bowls and top each portion with a dollop of whipped cilantro cream. Serve with potato beignets on the side.

Coriander-Dusted Potato Beignets

Makes about 40 small beignets

2 Tbsp (30 mL) ground coriander
½ cup (125 mL) buttermilk
1 egg
1 Tbsp (15 mL) butter, softened
1 cup (250 mL) hot mashed potato (about 2 medium potatoes)
5 cups (1.25 L) all-purpose flour
1 Tbsp (15 mL) baking powder
½ tsp (2 mL) table salt
Canola oil for deep-frying

1. In a small skillet over medium heat, toast the coriander until it is fragrant, about 2 minutes. Scrape the coriander into a shallow bowl. Set aside.

2. In a large bowl, beat together the buttermilk, egg and butter. When thoroughly mixed, add the hot potato and stir well until combined. (Do not overmix or the potatoes will become gluey.)

3. In a medium bowl, sift together the flour, baking powder and salt.

4. Fold the flour mixture into the potato mixture until well combined.

5. Turn the mixture onto a lightly floured surface. Knead lightly until smooth. Roll out to ½-inch (1 cm) thickness. Cut into rounds with a 1¼-inch (3 cm) cookie cutter.

6. Pour the oil into a large, deep saucepan to a depth of 3 inches (8 cm). Heat the oil to 350°F (180°C).

7. Fry the beignets in batches until lightly browned, 2 to 3 minutes.

8. With a slotted spoon, transfer to paper towels to drain, then toss in the toasted coriander. Serve at once.

Spot prawns are a sweet delicacy in B.C. They're wild, local and certified sustainable but the season isn't long, making them all the more desirable. Mission Hill's Select Lot Collection Chardonnay is the ideal accompaniment to the creamy richness of this bisque, which has enough weight to match the nice balance of the wine's oak and acidity. Potatoes and Chardonnay—what a combination!
—Matthew Batey

Yemenite Chicken Soup

Lisa Shamai, Soup Sister

Makes about 6 servings

Called *hawaij*, this is used in Israel to season everything from soups to stews.

1 Tbsp (15 mL) olive or coconut oil

8 skinless, bone-in chicken thighs

2 onions, coarsely chopped

2 carrots or 1 large sweet potato, peeled and coarsely chopped

2 Tbsp (30 mL) Yemenite spice mix (see below)

10 cups (2.5 L) water

3 potatoes, peeled and diced

2 zucchini or summer squash, coarsely chopped

2 tomatoes, cored and coarsely chopped

1 small head garlic, coarsely chopped

Salt and pepper to taste

Finely chopped cilantro or parsley for garnish (optional)

Lemon wedges for serving (optional)

When I lived in Israel, I enjoyed many Friday night dinners with a Yemenite family. This aromatic soup was often on the menu. I love it so much, I sometimes pare down the ingredients to make a quick, comforting dinner for one.

—Lisa Shamai

1. In a large pot, heat the oil over medium heat. Add the chicken thighs, onions, carrots and spice mix. Cook, stirring often, for 5 minutes.

2. Add the water, potatoes, zucchini, tomatoes and garlic. Bring to a boil.

3. Reduce the heat and simmer, covered, until the vegetables are tender, about 40 minutes. Season with salt and pepper to taste.

4. Ladle into bowls. Sprinkle with a flourish of cilantro (if using) and add a spritz of lemon juice (if using).

Yemenite Spice Mix

Makes about ½ cup (125 mL)

2 Tbsp (30 mL) pepper

2 Tbsp (30 mL) ground cumin

2 Tbsp (30 mL) turmeric

2 tsp (10 mL) ground cardamom

2 tsp (10 mL) ground coriander

2 tsp (10 mL) ground ginger

In a small bowl, stir together all the ingredients. Store in an airtight jar.

Zuppa di Pesce (Italian Fish Soup)

Nicole Gomes, Chef/Owner, Nicole Gourmet, Calgary

Makes about 4 servings

12 manila clams in their shells, scrubbed
2 Tbsp (30 mL) cornmeal
¼ cup (60 mL) olive oil
½ small onion, finely chopped
4 anchovy fillets, drained, rinsed and minced
3 cloves garlic, minced
1½ tsp (7 mL) red chili flakes
½ bunch parsley, finely chopped
1 lb (500 g) white fish fillet, such as snapper, cut into 1-inch (2.5 cm) pieces

Salt to taste
3 plum tomatoes, diced
¾ cup (185 mL) white wine
12 mussels in their shells, scrubbed
12 jumbo large shrimp, peeled and deveined
1 cup (250 mL) passata (see sidebar)
½ cup (125 mL) fresh basil leaves, torn or cut into strips
Extra virgin olive oil for drizzling

Passata is an Italian sauce made from puréed tomatoes. It's usually sold in jars. Look for it near the tomato sauce in your supermarket or in Italian grocery stores.

1. The day before making the soup, discard any clams that don't close when tapped sharply on the counter.

2. Put the remaining clams in a bowl and add enough cold water to cover them. Add the cornmeal and refrigerate overnight. Drain the clams well, then refrigerate until needed.

3. In a large pot, heat the oil over medium heat. Add the onion. Cook, stirring often, until the onion has softened but is not brown.

4. Add the anchovies, garlic and chili flakes. Cook, stirring, for 1 minute. Stir in the parsley.

5. Add the fish and season with salt to taste.

6. Add the tomatoes and reserved clams. Cook, stirring gently, for 1 minute.

7. Add the wine. Bring to a simmer and simmer for 1 minute.

8. Add the mussels (discarding any that don't close when tapped sharply on the counter), shrimp and passata. Cook, covered, until the shrimp are pink and the clams and mussels have opened, about 3 minutes. Discard any shellfish that haven't opened.

9. Add the basil and season with salt to taste.

10. Ladle up chunky bowlfuls and drizzle with extra virgin olive oil. Serve with grilled ciabatta.

Keep the Soup Flowing

Since Soup Sisters launched in 2009, tens of thousands of soup makers have gathered in commercial kitchens across the country for an evening of camaraderie that, to date, has produced more than 350,000 servings of soup. Each participant pays $55 to cover the cost of good-quality soup ingredients, a chef facilitator and a communal meal. Events can typically accommodate 20 to 30 participants whom we call Soup Sisters and Broth Brothers, women and men joining forces in the kitchen to take care of others one bowl at a time.

We have now developed some incredible programs within our organization to meet new needs and opportunities. In Canada, one in every three teens will experience abuse in their romantic relationships before they graduate from high school. Focusing on healthy relationships that foster respect for one another, Summer Stock takes place at summer camps throughout the country. Campers and counselors learn cooking skills and become young philanthropists in a hands-on, fun and meaningful way.

Prior to the soup making, a professional speaker or shelter representative talks to the teens about how to recognize the signs and symptoms of abuse, how to support a friend, where to get help, and how to stay safe on dates and social media. The soup they make is delivered to shelters near each participating camp.

The Big Stir is an annual event in Calgary that attracts hundreds of participants to a single venue for an evening of soup making and fun. This event gives Soup Sisters the opportunity to raise funds to help meet our demands for growth, ensure continued support of emergency shelters nationwide, and raise awareness about domestic abuse and family violence prevention.

The event produces more than 1,200 servings of soup for local women's shelters! Our typical shopping list for The Big Stir is as enormous and profoundly significant as the stand we take against domestic violence and family abuse:

- 127 qts (127 L) chicken stock
- 94 lb (43 kg) diced tomatoes
- 77 lb (35 kg) carrots
- 69 lb (31 kg) onions
- 51 lb (23 kg) chicken
- 161 cloves garlic
- 350 aprons
- 200 cutting boards
- 100 knives
- 25 gas burners
- 100 volunteers
- 25 professional chefs
- 1 paramedic

Our Soup Sisters Heart is a beautiful, one-of-a-kind piece of jewelry. Each handmade silver heart costs $220 and can be purchased on our website (soupsisters.org/heart.php). Most emergency shelters can accommodate women and children for three weeks before they either transition to a second-stage shelter or return home. When they leave the emergency shelter, they're given a few essential items. For each heart bought by a supporter, one is also given to a woman in transition as a symbol of hope as she moves on with her life.

Chickn Molé Soup

www.soupsisters.org

INGREDIENTS:

Chicken Mole Soup
Butter, Chicken & Stock, Mole
(Mexican chili chocolate spice),
Onion, Red pepper, garlic, Black
beans, corn, tomato, Cilantro

SOUP SISTERS

Made fresh: Sept 13 2010 By: Nicole, Dorothy & Hazel

It's More Than Just Soup:
What It Means to Be a Soup Sisters Volunteer

All across Canada I've had the wonderful privilege of meeting our amazing Soup Sisters volunteers, the core group of women in each chapter who ensure our soup-making events are fun for our supporters. They warm my heart with their passion.

Our volunteers have told me that taking care of others through soup "spoke to them" and encouraged them to start a Soup Sisters chapter in their own cities. Strong new friendships have blossomed, and they have a sense of personal ownership and stewardship of the organization's values.

Here, some of those volunteers share what Soup Sisters means to them:

"Back in 2009, during my first full year of early retirement, I found myself thinking that I should probably do something to give back to the community. I love to cook and I felt that if I were going to cook for anyone, it would be someone who really needed me. Flipping through *City Palate* magazine, I saw a blurb about Soup Sisters and sent an e-mail to Sharon offering my admin skills. Sharon shared her passion and vision, let me help her put it all into a nice format, and a dynamic team was born.

I love being a Soup Sister because there's not one thing I do that goes unappreciated, and it's nice to feel part of something so special. Everyone at Soup Sisters knows it's about so much more than soup. That comfort in a bowl represents the hope that things will get better with the support and strength of a caring community."
—*Carolyn Sainchuk, Calgary*

"Through the many stories I've heard from our shelter rep during our soup-making sessions, I've gained such respect for the strong women who finally make it to the shelter. These women should be applauded, supported and nurtured by their community.

Soup Sisters has been a tremendous gift in my life. The organization provides such a light-hearted way to share and give, which obviously resonates with so many in our community. Our Soup Sisters events in Kelowna are booked a year in advance! Every detail of this perfect program has been created so lovingly by our founder Sharon Hapton, right down to the handwritten labels on each soup container which add that extra touch of nurturing, as if the soups come from Mom or Grandma."
—*Jennifer Schell, Victoria*

"Knowing that I'm part of an ongoing support group helping women, children and youth rebuild a more positive life for themselves is immensely rewarding. I've learned that bad things can happen to good people from all walks of life. Domestic abuse, homelessness and addiction know no status—they affect everyone, regardless of race, religion or culture. But their victims don't need pity; they need comfort and support and a community that cares. Soup Sisters is the most rewarding volunteer work I have ever done, and it fills my heart to know that I am making a difference one bowl at a time."
—*Sheila Alwell, Vancouver*

"Being a Soup Sister has made me feel I make a tangible difference in the lives of women and children in my community. As the communications/event coordinator for Soup Sisters in London, Ontario, I help promote, organize and execute our monthly soup-making events. When people first arrive at the kitchen, there's excitement (and the smell of delicious appetizers!) in the air. After attendees enjoy some snacks and a glass of wine, a representative from our local women's shelter speaks about how their clients are often scared, isolated and so upset that they have little appetite. A warm bowl of soup, made by caring members of their own community, provides nourishing comfort for these families.

At this point, you can typically hear a pin drop as our Soup Sisters realize how meaningful their chopping, grating and stirring will be. Then we get to work! The kitchen becomes full of energy, chatter and beautiful aromas as we create three or four different soups. After sitting down to a delicious meal of some of our soup, the participants leave knowing they've been a part of something very special."
—*Alyson Nichols, London, ON*

"What brought me to Soup Sisters was the simple idea of making soup and nurturing someone in need of comfort. I love listening to the shelter representatives talk about the difference a bowl of soup can make. It's not just the soup, but rather the notion that somebody is caring enough to prepare it. I've heard many stories from the beneficiaries of the soup and seen many tears from participants when those stories are told. By participating in a Soup Sisters event, I feel like I'm actually touching someone's heart and helping in a way I can relate to."
—*Karen Miller, Calgary*

"In my professional career, I've worked with at-risk youth, women who've experienced abuse and men who've used violence on their partners. As a volunteer with Soup Sisters, I've been able to support my innovative and compassionate friend Sharon Hapton. Soup Sisters has also given my children a meaningful place to volunteer. There are many ways Soup Sisters has made a difference. Most importantly, we have been able to engage men in a nonthreatening, inclusive way. Soup Sisters helps educate them to support women and children on their journey to a violence-free life, and our events enable men to take a stand to end violence against women."
—*Lynne Oreck-Wener, Ottawa* (an inaugural Soup Sister who attended the first-ever Soup Sisters event, in Calgary in 2009)

"Volunteering has been scientifically proven to make you feel better about yourself. I think Soup Sisters goes a step further, enabling us to be involved with the soup's entire journey, from the evening's introduction through the chopping, stirring and labeling, to the delivery of the soup to the shelter. It's a win-win for everyone."
—*Lynnie Wonfor, Calgary* (an inaugural Soup Sister who attended the first-ever Soup Sisters event, in Calgary in 2009)

"When Soup Sisters participants come to make soup, they hear about the needs of members of the community who are at risk, and they start to think of other ways they can help. A music therapy program began this way. Others have made baby quilts, knitted sweaters and mitts, donated household items or offered to babysit. We were once invited to an elementary school where a social awareness club wanted to know how Soup Sisters worked. Afterward, they made soup in their school kitchen and donated it to their local shelter."
—*Sandi McCrory, Kitchener, ON*

"After reading about the inaugural Toronto Soup Sisters event in 2010, I booked an evening for a group of friends. We now have three events under our belts, more booked and, yes, we're serial soup makers! We've since been joined by daughters, sons, partners and in-laws, making our Soup Sisters evenings community-building family gatherings as well as an opportunity to spread awareness about abuse. My best guess is that, so far, we've made about 600 servings of soup...and counting!

Soon after my first Soup Sisters evening, I became a kitchen volunteer. It's been such a pleasure facilitating the events, ensuring that other groups enjoy the rewarding experience of cooking together and sharing a meal in support of women and children in need. I'm always humbled by the staff of Toronto's Interval House who speak with such passion about the services they provide for the women and children who seek shelter there. My heart aches when I think of the bravery of the women who take that huge step to escape their abusers.

Soup Sisters has really opened my eyes to the need in our communities to provide supportive, safe shelter for women and children living with abusive partners and to how soul soothing a simple bowl of soup can be when lives are in turmoil."
—*Marina Helwig-Ostler, Toronto*

"I've met some wonderful people through Soup Sisters. We have had a number of women who work at the shelters in Victoria come and talk to our group. One of them was a young woman in her 20s who told us what it was like living with an abusive father and the strength her mother needed to get the family out of that situation. Her honesty and compassion touched us all. Soup Sisters has restored my faith in volunteer organizations. Becoming a volunteer is an easy and meaningful way to do something that has a huge benefit for others."
—*Ginny Glover, Victoria, BC*

Broccoli Torte

Broccoli, tortellini, cheese, pasta sauce oregano, salt, pepper

Soup Sisters   Warming hearts
www.sou

Acknowledgments

The *Soup Sisters Cookbook* came out in 2012 and was an instant best-seller. Time has since flown, and the Soup Sisters and Broth Brothers organization continues to grow at a rapid pace. We believe that wherever there is a shelter for women and children fleeing domestic abuse, or a program for youth in crisis, there should be a Soup Sisters and Broth Brothers chapter.

It's a heart-breaking fact that shelters exist everywhere, in cities large and small. Fortunately, in those very same cities there are caring communities ready to lend a soup-making hand and provide a bottomless pot in more than one sense.

My thanks go to all of the chefs, food writers, Soup Sisters and Broth Brothers from across Canada and beyond who contributed to this incredible compilation of wholesome and nourishing soups. There seems to be no end to the gastronomic creativity of our many contributors, and this second book features more than 100 new soup recipes. Many include wonderful personal anecdotes that provide insight into the soups' history.

Soup is more than the sum of its parts. It's a meal that is intimately connected with the stories of our lives. Such tales take hold of our imaginations and emotions in ways that expand beyond a humble soup's nutritional benefits. Mothers tell us stories of family celebrations around a big dinner table. Young people recall eating soup made by a caring grandma or an understanding aunt who took special care of them at a vulnerable time.

To the thousands who unite at our soup-making events, sharing laughter, camaraderie and cooking skills to create new soup memories and stories of their own, I thank you for your time and generosity of spirit.

My amazing family continues to support my soup-driven obsession. While it means that Soup Sisters vies for my attention at times, we agree that this epic soup journey has been a good experience for all of us.

Thank you to my dear children, Dan and Blaire, who motivated me to create a caring organization to fill the giant "nurture void" left when they set off on their own adventures. You are both very patient with your soup-talking mother and often offer me the wisdom and advice that can only come from people who know my heart and honor my path.

Garry, my sweet, kind husband and the awesome father to our children, you define support and there is no question Soup Sisters would not have come to be without your generosity, pride and encouragement. You provide constructive criticism, unbounded love and guilt-free time that lets me focus on an ever-growing social enterprise. As soon as this cookbook goes to print, I'm writing a thank-you letter to the creators of *Candy Crush* for providing hours of husband-absorbing entertainment.

The pages of this book are graced by Julie Van Rosendaal's photography and food styling. It is an incredible honor to have Julie support both books. She is the busiest woman on the planet but still finds time to be enthusiastic, and does everything with humor and heartfelt generosity.

Our cover photograph was shot, once again, by the amazing Shallon Cunningham who also volunteers her time and expertise to Soup Sisters and Broth Brothers. We are truly privileged to have the gifts and talents of both women on display in this book.

To shoot the 48 beautiful soup pictures, we required a small army of volunteers to make the recipes for Julie to photograph. Employees of Calgary's "souper," socially responsible companies Nexen Energy ULC and Cenovus Energy were given a day off to help us get the job done. They chopped all day with Cutco chef knives generously donated for The Big Stir. We are eternally grateful to all of them for their ongoing support of Soup Sisters and Broth Brothers.

Photos from Soup Sisters events were contributed by volunteer photographers Garth Anderson, Annemarie Grudën Photography, Tyler Chan, Tom Irwin, Leap Photographic, Niles High Photography and Salt Food Photography.

Robert McCullough, Lindsay Paterson and Lucy Kenward from Appetite by Random House have my eternal gratitude for their gentle yet sure guidance, encouragement and practical know-how in producing this second beautiful book. They are an awesome team and I feel incredibly privileged to have had their support.

Julia Aitken has once again edited the recipes with her special flair. It is comforting to be able to trust an editor completely and know she understands what I am trying to say when my own words are not cooperating.

Dorothy Sitek of Generation Communications in Vancouver understands Soup Sisters and Broth Brothers intuitively, is a valuable source of smart, creative ideas and can always be counted on to edit my writing without compromising my voice.

"Souper" thanks also go to managing editor Susan Burns at Random House of Canada, to Leah Springate for designing the cover, and to copyeditor Naomi Pauls.

Finally, my deepest thanks go out to the heart of the organization, the volunteers across the country who ensure that the soups get made and delivered each month and have helped define the meaning of a "hug in a bowl." All the Soup Sisters and Broth Brothers I have come to know and care for so deeply take delight in taking care of others in the simplest and most heartfelt way. You are the essential ingredients of the organization and the ultimate recipe for kindness, generosity and passion.

Index